UNTOLD STORIES

Remembering Clydebank in Wartime

Clydebank Life Story Group

ACKNOWLEDGEMENTS

This book is published with financial assistance from:
Clydebank Trust
West Dunbartonshire Council.
Alexander Cross Cameron Fund
Awards for All

The publishers would like to thank Clydebank Central Library for kind permission to use photographs, and also Faber and Faber for permission to reprint an extract from *Burnt Norton, Four Quartets* from *Collected Poems 1909-1966* by T.S. Eliot.

Clydebank Life Story Group would like to thank the following for help and encouragement in bringing the book to publication: Jean Allan, Clydebank Citizens' Advice Bureau, Wynn Conway, Morison Memorial Church, Alison Miller, Alex McNair, James McNeill J.P., Marion Nimmo.

ISBN 0 9535172 0 9

Published February 1999 by
CLYDEBANK LIFE STORY GROUP

Seventh printing, 2006.

Cover Design by The Graphics Company

Edited by Liam Stewart
Printed by Clydeside Press

CONTENTS

Introduction

Time present and time past
Are both perhaps present in time future,
And time future contained in time past.

T.S. Eliot

'Untold Stories' began life in an autobiography-writing class in Clydebank College. When recalling their childhoods, a number of the participants found that they were tapping into the same seam – the war years in Clydebank. The idea of making a collection of such memoirs and inviting as many people as possible to contribute grew quickly. Such a collection had not been made before, Denis Kearns assured us, and there was so much to tell. (Indeed, as we go to press, people are still sending their stories or the names of people we should contact for volume two). So Clydebank Life Story Group was born.

Betty Moore, whose quiet dignity had moved us all so much as she told the story of her own terrible loss and the bleak aftermath, was another inspiration. The revelation that she had never written of her experiences before was a further impetus, and perhaps a source of the title of the book.

We also had the good fortune to have as a member of the group Helen McNeill, whose work in connection with the commemoration of the Clydebank Blitz has gained renown far beyond the local area. A very large proportion of the material in the book (including stories from overseas) is there because of Helen's prodigious energy and the success of a project she had already initiated.

A fellow Blitz Memorial Committee member is Denis Kearns. In her second piece in this book, Helen gives an account of how the committee came into being because a number of Clydebank's citizens could not live with the Council's decision to end the annual Blitz Memorial Service. Denis's conviction on this issue is unflinching. If Clydebank is to continue as a community worth being part of, it has to hold this vital part of its history carefully, like precious water, in both hands. To the book project, Denis has brought this seriousness of purpose as well as a wide and detailed knowledge of the history of the area.

But, of course, the book is not a history. It is a gathering point, a place where people can bring their memories and their feelings about their encounters with life and death all those years ago, and reflect on how they have come through them. Statistical accuracy can be obtained from other sources. Still, it was with her astonishingly detailed recall that Agnes Watson provided the group with so much stimulation and pleasure. What she remembers with great vividness are the human details which so effectively recreate the life and community of the past. The precious wartime gift of chocolate came in a block of exactly thirty two squares, thirty two obvious opportunities in the eyes of Agnes's parents, to share the pleasure of the chocolate with friends and neighbours. Thus is the collectivism of those years remembered and brought back to life!

Isa McKenzie does something similar in describing the coat she put on as she left the house about to be destroyed in the Blitz. 'It was a dusky, pink material, with brown fur around the neck and down to the waist. It was fastened by a button at the waist and a toggle-shaped cloth strap at the neck........it was one of the loveliest things I ever had.' It is as if the coat becomes a symbol of the time and place that was destroyed, and her ability to remember it in detail, some guarantee that not everything was lost. Isa was a later recruit to the group but quickly became an enthusiastic supporter of the project.

Two other members, Deirdre Craig and June Galloway who were neither from Clydebank nor old enough to remember the war, nonetheless took an active part in the project, willingly accepting that concentration on this book has meant a temporary suspension of the group's wider autobiographical activities. In practical matters relating to the creation of a book, Deirdre's experience in library publishing has been invaluable. June, who is the chairperson of the group, has made wise comments on many aspects of the production, as well as being an active gatherer of material on an outreach basis.

Some of the recollections and stories we received were based on taped conversations but most were in the form of the written word, and much of it handwritten, a phenomenon which somehow created more of a sense of direct communication with the authors. The cover design incorporates a section of the pages of copper-plate submitted by James Wotherspoon who, at ninety-nine, is one of the oldest contributors.

Have we ended up with a book of the 'where were you on those nights' variety? Partly. And that is perhaps what gives the collection its poignancy. But there is much more than that. For instance, there are the sharply varied descriptions of the evacuations, ranging from Denis Kearns's near idyllic experience at Hill House in Helensburgh, through the risible class snobberies remembered by V.M., to the sadness of Betty Moore's exile in Blantyre. There are also wider reflections on what it was like to be a child at that time, reflections, for instance about the fragility of innocence and the vague awareness of the strange adult world. People also diverge in their views about post-disaster trauma and other psychological scars. For some, not enough was done for those who suffered; others see the absence of such initiatives as testimony to the greater resilience of the time

However, it is the experience, of the nights of the Blitz which predominates. In presenting this, one of the governing principles has been inclusiveness. In 1997, Helen McNeill sat in the Clydebank Museum and created a tapestry of the town's coat of arms, a tapestry to which anyone could add a stitch if they wished to commemorate someone who died in the Blitz. People were not rejected on the basis that their loss fell outwith Clydebank. If they found the context appropriate, they added their stitch. This principle we have extended to the book. So there are some contributors whose memories of the bombings relate to places around Clydebank, James McBride, for instance, now a Clydebank resident, whose piercing story of the 14th March, tells of the night his family was destroyed in a single end in Maryhill. There is also one from Greenock and again, we have accommodated the writer's need to add her stitch of remembrance. Maybe more such communal artistic creations are needed to provide people with outlets for their stories and memories.

But overwhelmingly, the book recreates Clydebank at the time of the Blitz. The place names recur again and again: Jellicoe street, Napier Street, Second Avenue, Boquhanran School, John Brown's, Singer's, The Regal, the La Scala. We can almost make a map of the town. Each story is different but patterns emerge: the moonlit night, people making their way along Kilbowie Road to the pictures or the dancing; the sirens, mothers and children in tenement closes and shelters; men clawing at the rubble of their former homes; everybody stumbling about the town, trying to find out who was alive, who was dead.

It was at the suggestion of the final member of the group, Nancy Clunas, that this introduction is pre-fixed by the quotation from T.S.Eliot. For Nancy, who comes from a Humanist and C.N.D. background, remembering the war means remembering all wars. In her own writing outwith this book she often adopts a sardonically humorous persona who has a way of taking the reader past superficialities to real human values. Her conviction that the past must be seen as saying something about the present is deep and unshakeable.

Indeed, writing this introduction in the immediate aftermath of a bombing raid on Iraq, I have the feeling that the relevance of these stories to here and now events is inescapable. For all political leaders, perhaps the last piece in the book, the account by Ann Holmes of the destruction of the Rocks family, should be compulsory reading. It is a story which records the horrors of war in honest and harrowing detail.

Nevertheless, though in this collection perhaps the sadness outweighs the humour, and though much of the material is painful, the book is offered as a celebration. In Ann Holmes's story, such is the passion with which she recalls the bombing of 78 Jellicoe Street, that the people she writes about, Walter Greig, Annie Rocks, John Rocks, are celebrated and live again. In the same way, others are brought to life in dozens of vignettes throughout the book, people like John McCusker and Albert Bowman, and so many nameless mothers who held on to their families and endured the nights of bombing, then searched ruined streets for a means of survival.

The book is a record of their humanity, and a celebration of the great human values of kindness, courage, endurance and love.

Liam Stewart
Clydebank College

Clydebank Lifestory Group
Back Lto R: Deirdre Craig, Nancy Clunas, Isa McKenzie, Denis Kearns, June Galloway.
Front : Agnes Watson, Betty Moore, Helen McNeill

Elizabeth Bailey

ESTHER

Esther, my school friend, spent the early evening of the 13th March 1941 playing street games with myself and other children near my home. She had come straight home with me from school. We all had the most exciting fun, running and jumping; it was a taste of summer soon to come, as it always did with all our childish pursuits. Little did we know our childhood days were over.

I remember there was the most beautiful of sunsets in the sky away down the River Clyde above the dark rock of Dumbarton where the ancient castle stands. The weather being so mild we played on much later than usual. I then went with Esther to see her to the bus for her short journey home. It was just too late for her to walk; I normally walked part of the way with her. The bus drove off. A smile, a wave. 'See you tomorrow.'

By a lapse of memory, she left her schoolbag and gas mask in my home. How terrible it would have been if there had been a gas attack. She would have her bag in the morning, so everything would, of course, be alright; we were not going to have any gas attacks, we were not going to have any part of the war. My childish mind had sorted it all out.

It was around nine o'clock when the sirens sounded. I was catching up on my home work and wanted to finish it. It would be another false alarm. My mother seemed more alarmed than I had seen her before and we were all rushed into the Anderson shelter – the searchlights were already in the sky, the rumble of guns not so far off. This was going to be a nightmare night. Mum, my two young sisters, my baby brother, our widowed neighbour and our little spaniel Maisie, all crushed down as quickly as we tumbled in.

I was so stiff in the morning when the raids were over. But we were all very lucky to be alive. My dad was on nightshift on the other side of the Clyde. It must have been dreadful for Mum with all the responsibility, but I did not think that way at the time. Dad spent the night in horror as he watched with all the other men in the factory the German planes coming in on waves of raids, dropping hundreds of bombs on Clydebank. There were rumours that the whole of the population had been wiped out, he told us when he finally made his way home through the debris and road blocks. He arranged that we move out immediately.

I found out months later that Esther was killed. She lived in a tenement house on the hill above Singer's factory. So many of these houses had direct hits and were razed to the ground, causing a terrible loss of life. Esther's dad also lost his life.

When much later, I purchased I.M.M.MacPhail's 'The Clydebank Blitz', I remember how surprised I was to read in the 'List of Fatal Casualties' that Esther's dad was only 33 years old (only 20 when Esther was born). I never heard her talk of her mother and as a child I did not think to ask, although I was much aware of the fact. She did seem to have an aunt in the house as I vaguely recollect.

I would like to add this little poem as a memory of Esther.

To Esther with Love, Betty

It was Good-night under a setting sun
With all the joy of years to come
Before the dawn terror tore the sky
You to die; I to cry
For our sweet Good-night
Was a sad Good-bye.

Elizabeth Bailey 1943.

Nancy Clunas

DIARY OF A CHILD EVACUEE SIX MONTHS BEFORE THE BLITZ

Sunday 13/9/40

Miss Jackson says we should all write a diary on the day it is our birthday, to record what we are doing and thinking about that day. Today I am 10, and Charlie gave me 'Alice in Wonderland' and wrote inside it 'Happy Birthday, Flora, 1940.' I love that book. Daddy came over from Dalmuir yesterday, and Daddy, Mum and I went to the Globe to see Betty Grable and Carmen Miranda in 'Carnival in Costa Rica.' Picturegoer has pictures of Betty's Hollywood home, high in the Hollywood hills. Betty has on her bathing costume, ready to jump into the big swimming pool. Her husband, Harry James, is standing with his head back, playing the trumpet. Charlie is away out with Johnny, Charlie and Neil on their bikes. He says Betty is not a patch on Rita Hayworth, but I love Betty. That John Payne is a bit wishy-washy. I think Betty would be better off with Don Ameche, but he is just a good friend and owns the nightclub where Betty and Carmen work. Betty has a lot of worries over all John Payne's girlfriends that he forgets to tell her about. But Carmen gives her a good talking to and then cheers her up by singing 'Chick Chick A Boom, Chick A Boom.' Mum says not to worry, cos love is blind and, anyway, everybody's taste is different.

Charlie, Daddy and I took Nan's dog (Gyp) a good long walk up through the Bluebell woods this morning. Gyp loves it and nearly goes mad when we knock Nan's door for him.

They took the palings off the Thorn School and Johnstone public park to make Spitfires. I hate those Nazis. It said in the paper 'Paris falls without a Fight,' and the pictures showed all the soldiers marching through that big arch, and another soldier riding beside them on a horse. Mum says to watch and not empty the tealeaves over the potato peelings, because the food for the pigs collected in the brock pail should not include tea leaves.

Must finish off now because Ethel is coming up for me. We are going to go over our song for the class concert on Friday. We were going to do Carmen Miranda's song. 'Aye, aye, aye, aye, aye, I like you very much, aye, aye, aye, aye, aye I think you're grand,' but it is not in the McLennan Song Book I bought in Woolworth's (6d). So we are just going to sing, 'Don't sit under the apple tree with any one else but me.' We practised it on Friday going down the Thorn Brae from school. We went to Grannie's and Auntie Chrissie took us to the park. There are three Andrews sisters and only two of us, so we just had to sing that bit louder. Auntie Chrissie says we are better than the Andrews sisters, and shoved us away high up on the swings.

Today we are going to the Clock Café to sit in and have 'oyster sundae,' that is ice cream with raspberry over it and a sponge biscuit. Now that Ethel and I are both ten years of age, we like to do that on a Sunday, rather than just eat a pokey hat in the street.

The Day War Broke Out

As the broadcast ended, Flora looked up at her father and mother, sitting with her at the kitchen table. Her father, his face serious, reached over and switched off the wireless. They were sitting in silence. 'We are now at war with Germany,' Mr Chamberlain had said. Flora wondered what would happen now. Her mother got up suddenly and went out of the kitchen. Daddy looked down at Flora, smiled and said encouragingly, 'Would you like to go out to play for a wee while?'

Flora gazed up at him, wonderingly. Had he forgotten this was Sunday? You did not go out to play on a Sunday. You either went over to Granny's at Johnstone or went for a walk with Mum and Daddy. If it was raining, you stayed in and either played or read in the big room. 'Just until your dinner's ready,' Daddy said. He was very keen that she should go out this Sunday. Flora felt uneasy. Where was Mum anyway? If she had just gone to the lavatory, she was taking an awful long time. But perhaps some of her pals would be out playing. Flora decided to do as Dad suggested. She could not make head nor tail of it. It was just one of those occasions when adults behaved very oddly. She grabbed her coat and ran downstairs to the high back.

Brambling: Nancy Clunas, Richard McGregor and Charles Clunas

Douglas, Graham and Vera were already there, but there was no running about or playing that day. They just stood beside the palings talking about what was going to happen. Flora knew that Mussolini's army and airforce were fighting against the Abyssinians, who were poor people. 'Bombing barefoot natives who are fighting with bows and arrows,' she had heard Daddy say. Now this country was at war with Germany. Flora wondered what that would be like. At the Pictures, they had seen on the news the German planes divebombing and machine-gunning people in Spain. 'A rehearsal for the bigger war to come,' it said in The Daily Worker and The News Chronicle. Flora had felt sick with fear as she watched the terrified people trying to run to safety. One woman was clutching a wee baby as she ran.

'We're going to stay at uncle Will's at Johnstone,' Flora told Graham and Douglas, who were talking about going to be evacuated.

Graham's mother lifted the window to call him in for his dinner. Then Flora heard her mother shouting on her. She ran upstairs and into the house, and hurried to sit down beside Daddy at the table. Mum was bustling about, dishing up the meat and potatoes. 'M-m-m, lovely gravy,' breathed Flora, eagerly tucking into her dinner, her former worries forgotten.

Betty Moore

THE NIGHT THAT CHANGED MY LIFE

It was a night like any other; children were making the most of the last ten minutes of their play before being called in for the night. Betty and her friends were playing at skipping ropes whilst David, her brother, played with the boys on their bikes.

'Five minutes to go you two,' called their mother, 'then upstairs.' Once in the house, David had homework to do, then the nightly chore of cleaning both his and Betty's shoes for the next day. Betty's chore was setting the table for the next morning's breakfast. Then they got washed, changed into their night clothes, and into bed. They both slept in the recess bed in the room, their mother and father in the recess bed in the kitchen, with a cot for Robert, the baby. Betty loved this little boy and was so proud when allowed to push him in the lovely new pram. She was the envy of all her friends.

Part of the family routine every evening was to make sure heavy clothes were left at hand, flasks were filled and gas masks ready to lift if there was an air raid. David had a heavy tweed coat, and Betty a teddy-bear fur coat. Both had seen better days but were very warm.

It hardly seemed any time at all had passed before the awful wail of the siren wakened them. Up they got, quickly donned their heavy clothes, and then settled themselves down to await the all-clear when they could get back to bed.

The noise was somewhat louder this evening, but they were all cosy and not too concerned. Then this awful din. Someone was banging on the door. Betty's mother opened it and there stood the ARP warden. 'You'll have to go down into the back close. It's really bad out there.'

They all trooped downstairs and joined the other families. There were two long benches on either side of the wall for the parents to sit on, while the children sat on mats on the floor. There wasn't much room, but all squeezed in and got as comfortable as they could.

Suddenly Betty remembered Robert's pram. It had been left out in the backcourt for her father to bring in when he came home from working late in the shipyard. She spoke to her mother about this, and suggested, as she was not very big, perhaps she could crawl out into the backcourt and rescue the pram (obviously not thinking how it would get into this crowded place).

Just then there was an almighty bang, and all the lights were blown out, doors were crashing, windows smashing. Nobody could see what was happening. The children by this time were crying for the parents they could no longer see because of the darkness. Betty grabbed hold of somebody's hand, hoping it might be David's. Another loud bang and a terrible rumbling sound, screaming – then SILENCE.

How long Betty had been lying there she did not know. All she was aware of was she could not move, she was jammed under something very heavy. She tried calling out, but nothing happened.

After a very long time (five and a half hours she later learnt) she was aware of a loud clanging sound not so far away. Gruff voices – what could be going on?!

'Just lie still, hen. We'll get you out.' Then more shouting. 'Teddy-bear coat did the man say? Aye, that's what it is.' More clanging, then there was a hint of daylight. Someone was trying very hard to get her out.

The next thing she saw was the grief-stricken face of her father as he was handed the bundle in the teddy-bear coat. 'I've got you Betty, you'll be just fine.'

As she was being moved into the waiting ambulance, Betty caught hold of her father's sleeve. 'The pram, Daddy,' she said. 'Did you get the pram?'

THE AFTERMATH

Some time during the day of Friday 14th March 1941, my father and I arrived at the home of my grandparents in Anniesland. Very soon after, I was put into the recessed bed in the kitchen. Everybody was talking in low whispering voices, and the outside door seemed to be continually opening and closing as members of the family started arriving, each one trying to be so brave, but without any success. Eventually I must have fallen asleep, and in no time at all was being wakened by my grandfather as the all too familiar wailing of the siren once again filled me with a terrible fear. This time I was carried off to an air-raid shelter where I was comforted by my grandparents. How long this lasted I have no idea. My memory has been completely wiped out.

I remember attending school at Anniesland for a very short time, as I was soon on my way to Port Bannatyne, which is just outside Rothesay. My grandmother's sisters had holiday houses there, and it was felt both my grandparents and I had to get away from Glasgow. My mother's younger sister Anne accompanied us on this trip.

These were quite happy times with my mother's family coming at weekends whenever possible. I attended school there for another short time (this would be school number four).

We eventually returned to Anniesland. My grandmother was not at all well. She never really recovered from the shock resulting from the Blitz. My father meanwhile was trying to arrange a more permanent home for me away from Clydeside. He had a distant relative in Blantyre and it was arranged I go there. How this came about I don't know, but this started the unhappiest time of my life.

These people were complete strangers to me. There was a husband and wife and their son, his two boys and a bachelor son. Attendance at school number five was soon arranged, as were my daily duties in the house, these being I would set the table for all the meals, clear up after meals, wash and dry the dishes, keep the furniture dusted and, when required, get any shopping. Only then could I do my school homework. I never protested at bedtime. I was so tired I was grateful for the break.

Although I was doing quite well at school, nobody showed any interest, and even when my name was put forward to represent the school in a writing competition, no-one wanted to know. This competition covered the whole of Lanarkshire, and I was over the moon when I won. I was to be presented with my prize on prize giving day. I asked if anybody would be coming that day, but was told nobody had any time, and anyway, anyone could write a composition. I consoled myself by thinking the school hall would be so busy no-one would notice. But I knew I was alone.

After the summer holidays I was to start secondary school which was some distance away. I stayed in High Blantyre and the school was in Low Blantyre. It would take me a good twenty minutes to briskly walk there. I could either do Languages or Commercial. I opted for the latter, and for the first time, I felt I was doing something for my future. I fell in love with Mr Pitmann's Shorthand, and vowed I'd show them. Here was something they knew nothing about; it was a complete mystery to them.

One Saturday, when I went to bring the coal upstairs from the cellar in the backcourt, I discovered to my dismay the coalman had delivered that day, and the coal was all in big lumps, much too big for the fire, even if I had managed to fit it into the pail. I had to break it up. No hammer of course, so I thought if I dropped it on the ground it would break and I could lift the pieces on to the shovel – no waste. It was all working well, the coal breaking nicely with very little mess. Just then, I caught sight of Jenny, the woman looking after me. She had come down to the bin and, seeing my method of breaking the coal, nearly went berserk. She was carrying a brush and this she took over my back with such fury. How I got away from her flailing hands I don't know, but I rushed up the stairs and threw myself weeping sorely on to the bed, every bone aching.

I heard her come in the house carrying the pail. She banged the door closed, completely ignoring me. Later on I heard her setting the table. The family came home for tea and carried on with their meal. What excuse she gave for my absence I'll never know. There and then I made up my mind I had had enough.

Every Saturday evening the family would settle down in front of the fire and eagerly await the Saturday night play on the radio. I very rarely joined them. Instead I took myself off to the bedroom where I enjoyed reading my library book without fear of interruption. I heard the radio coming on and could imagine them all listening intently.

I had decided to run away and this was the best opportunity I'd get.

I found my suitcase, crammed my clothes in, found the pocket money I had hidden away every week, and slipped out the front door very quietly. Outside the streets were quite deserted for a Saturday night. I knew I had to get down the road to Low Blantyre where I would get a bus for Glasgow. I often wonder how I managed to carry a suitcase and walk that distance as quickly as I did, realising if I were to be missed I would have to be as far away from High Blantyre as possible, should anyone come looking for me.

I had to get a number 57 bus to Glasgow Waterloo Street. From there I would get a Balloch bus to my father, who was staying with his brother in Yoker. Had I taken the time and thought things out, I don't think I'd have gone through with my plan, but, given the circumstances that had led up to this action, I just had to try and get away from that awful house.

I boarded the almost empty bus, and told the conductress where I was going. Suspiciously she questioned me, but somehow I managed to convince her my father was expecting me at the other end.

At Waterloo Street Bus Station I soon found my way to the stance for the Balloch bus. The conductor explained to me that, as Yoker Mill Road was the Glasgow boundary, nobody could alight before then. However, he had a word with the driver who agreed to let me off before the boundary.

Having safely arrived, I then thought what my father would say to me. I would have to wait for a while yet, as, when I rang my uncle's door bell, I discovered there was nobody home.

Trailing the suitcase behind me, blinded by tears, I decided to sit it out at the mouth of the close and wait for my father to come home. Eventually, I heard somebody coming towards the close. The man glanced down at me and walked on. But then, he turned back. 'Are you alright?' he said. As I looked up at the face, he said, quietly and with disbelief, 'Is that you Betty?' Recognising my uncle, I threw myself into his arms and sobbed with relief. He lifted my suitcase and got me up the stair and into the safety of the house.

While I drank a cup of hot chocolate and ate some toast, I poured out my sorry tale. He assured me that, at least for that night, I would be staying and, while we waited for my father, a bed was prepared for me.

When my father arrived home, he could hardly believe his eyes. Yet again I was to relate my tale. By this time, of course, both men realised there must be more to all this. A trip to Blantyre had to be made right away. I never did learn what took place there.

During the ensuing week some lengthy discussions were necessary to decide what was to be done with me. I was quite happy to remain where I was. I realised if I were to stay, I would have to do my own laundry and share some of the household duties, and this would have to be fitted in with schoolwork. It was agreed to give it a trial.

After a few months, the lady who came to do the stair-washing had to give it up and, wishing to keep things running well, I volunteered to take this duty on. One Friday after school, I decided to start early before the stairs got too busy with workers arriving home for the evening. I was a bit shy of being seen by anyone, However, I had not bargained for children. Coming across this stranger, they wondered where I had come from. I had to laugh when one child said, ‘Who’s she?’

‘Oh,’ said her friend, knowingly, ‘She’s the girl with two daddies.’ What an apt description!

Life for me was a bit hectic, but I was a much happier person and felt I could cope with whatever life in future held for me. After all, wasn’t I the girl with two daddies.

Bessie Bannister

ORPHEUS CHOIR

I lived in the Parkhall area of Clydebank. The sirens sounded somewhere about mid-evening and we thought it would just be the usual: the sirens, then after a while the all-clear would sound and nothing would have happened. We were quite complacent. However, this time it was very different. As I had been ill with a very bad flu and I hadn't been out, we didn't go down to the shelter (an Anderson shelter in the garden) and that was something I'll always be thankful for, because by not going down to the garden shelter our lives were saved. In the morning, the shelter was devoid of all the sandbags and all the protection and sitting, full of boulders, on the edge of a huge crater. So obviously, had we been in the shelter, every one of us would have been killed, as did happen to people in other shelters

It was a great shock to the whole town. But the people of Clydebank really were tremendous, because ordinary people fought these incendiaries in a way that could never be forgotten. And the camaraderie of people helping one another in the next two days was something that I will never forget.

On the Friday evening,twenty six of us went to Callander in a coal lorry. I had an aunt in Callander who was on the home farm of an estate and she put everybody up, all twenty six from that coal lorry. When I think back, it's something quite funny I remember. I had received a fur coat for my twenty first birthday and the one thing I wanted to retrieve out of this Blitz was my fur coat. So I went to Callander with a face as black as coal, hands as black as coal and a fur coat!

The anti-aircraft guns in the Kilpatrick Hills also caused damage that night. Every time they were fired, the windows all shattered and doors flew off, and there was a lot of shrapnel from them as well. I think the very beginning of this was a night in February in the clear moonlight (I was in Glasgow that night) when the sirens sounded and this lone raider had come over and dropped flares. The local people thought that that was really when the damage was done. And also the A82, which we called the Boulevard, just shone like a ribbon and local people wondered if they had mistaken that for the river and that's why so much fell on the housing.

After the war, I went to Germany with the Orpheus Choir. I had thought that Clydebank had experienced everything that could happen but the sheer devastation of Germany shocked me. From Hamburg right up the Elbe across that part of Germany where the British army of the Rhine were, there was just nothing. The Allies had really done their work. We landed at Cuxhaven which was alright because it was a different area, and from there we had to take a train up to Hamburg. While we were in Cuxhaven, one of the most moving experiences we had was when we went to an officers' transit camp (we were in ENSA uniform). Sir Hugh, the boss as we called him, always asked us to sing to the waiters and waitresses wherever we went. So, when we went into this dining room (it was all German civilian population who were attending to us) he just stood up and said, 'We'll sing the Brahms.' And we sang Silent Night. Immediately these people all just stopped and tears were streaming down their faces. One of our wags in the choir said, 'Surely we're not as bad as all that!' But it was because they hadn't been allowed to listen to music like that during the war years. They were so moved by it, and it was a moment that endeared them to us

But the devastation of Hamburg was really something that I could never forget. The train was going very slowly because everything was just a mass of rubble and the train was more or less picking its way through. And running alongside the train were all these displaced people. We had all been given rations, a kind of packed meal, for the journey, and I remember the boss coming round all the compartments and telling us that not one of us was to eat that food. We were to throw it out to these people.

As we came into Hamburg, it was springtime and the place was covered in lilac trees growing among all this sheer devastation. But the smell of Hamburg could never be forgotten, because the dead were still underneath the rubble.

The big railway station was still there, very badly battered, and just across from it in a building that had once been a hotel there was the ENSA headquarters and an officers' transit camp with a NAAFI restaurant alongside it. We stayed there for ten days while we were doing our performances (we had a coach for personnel and a smaller one for all our luggage), and every day, while we were there, people came with bunches of lilac because they were so pleased. The concerts weren't supposed to be for German civilians, but, once they heard about the choir, they couldn't be kept out.

I remember one incident, when I had left my dirty uniform and I had gone back expecting to wash it myself, but found it wasn't there. When I went back in the evening, there it was laundered and my shoes were brushed. So when we found the girl who had done this, we asked her what we could do for her and she asked us just to give her a wee slice of our soap. So, of course, we gave her cakes of soap. But we found they were wonderful girls and they would have done anything for us.

Anne Fielding (née Macdonald)

THE BLITZ AND BEYOND

In 1941 I was nine years old. I had lived since I was nine months old in the top flat at number five Hill Street, Radnor Park. An only child, I was happy and secure in a caring, close-knit, working class community, where neighbours were trusted friends. I attended Boquhanran school, I was in the Brownies and every Sunday I could be found at Boquhanran Parish Church Sunday School. The war had intruded briefly into my life when, with some of my peers, I was evacuated to Arrochar. This evacuation had seemed at first more of an adventure than a wrenching away from the bosom of my family. Soon, however, loneliness and the stark reality of my situation began to cloud the initial euphoria. After three weeks my mother visited for the third time and was appalled at my neglected state. Home I came. After a hot bath and an assault on my hair with Derbac soap and a fine-toothed comb, I assumed my normal appearance!

Life, therefore, was now on a more or less even keel. The blackout curtains were in place, the suitcase, packed with the family papers and a few clothes, stood four-square at the outside door, while gas-mask drill had been practised so assiduously that it was second nature to us. We had become accustomed to the siren's wail. No danger had yet befallen us. Indeed, we children always hoped secretly that the alert would last longer than two hours, as that meant non-attendance at school the next morning!

Just when we had become somewhat blasé that unimaginable train of events started, at approximately 9p.m. on March 13th. Our response to the siren was automatic, almost nonchalant, so accustomed had we become to the routine. My father was critically ill (I was kept in the dark as to how ill he really was) but my mother and I hurried downstairs to the home of our neighbours in the 'middle' flat. Gradually the forced joviality of the adults petered out. It had become evident that a new element had entered the alert: it was much noisier and much more menacing than previously experienced by us. We should be safer on the ground floor flat, in the close, was the consensus of opinion. Once settled again, someone opened the bathroom door. Everyone gasped as we watched the Terraces, Second and Third, crumpling like a pack of cards. Next, the windows of the flat were blown out by the blast from a nearby bomb. The glass of the fanlight above the main door shattered, showering slivers of glass down on us, many embedding themselves in my mother's neck. The younger children screamed in terror; for some reason I was mute.

With the morning came the all-clear. We trooped upstairs. My father was fine, but oh! my poor mother's scrupulously clean house was a shambles. Soot and glass were everywhere. In the street outside, the scene was one of devastation. The houses on the opposite side of the street were ablaze and the glass was ankle-deep. I knew instantly what Hell would be like. The minister and the Sunday School teachers had described Hell to us and this surely matched the description. I thought to myself, 'I'll have to be good or I'll go to Hell.' I remember bargaining with God. 'Please, God, don't send me to Hell. Don't let us die. I'll be good. I'll go for the messages and help polish the brasses, if You will save us.' The incongruity of these promises did not occur to me. I had never polished the brasses and went only on a rare errand, because my mother had to budget very carefully every week. In any case, would the brasses ever require polishing again and which shop would be open! The child in me was simply endeavouring to bring normality where there was none.

During the Friday, as it now was, a neighbour came to sit with my father and me, while my mother scoured the district for an ambulance to take my father to hospital. Although, I knew none of this at the time, it transpired that she had to plead with policemen to be allowed access to streets where unexploded bombs were being monitored. An ambulance would definitely come, she was assured. By teatime, no ambulance had been forthcoming. My mother was distraught, but my father insisted that we must go to the school at Janetta Street to be evacuated. The neighbour's wife and son came with us; the two men stayed behind.

Exhausted, hungry and grimy, we joined the sad queue. I had seen only a smoking ruin where my beloved Boquhanran School once stood. It was too much! Worse was to come – there would be no transport. Some one had blundered. Into the school basement we trailed, to face an interminable night. Women all around were praying aloud, strange frightening incantations such as we never prayed in Boquhanran Church. These were simply 'set' prayers, but the fervour and intensity of the women scared me.

In the morning, Saturday, my mother was frantically buttonholing every warden in sight. Nobody knew anything about the ambulance service, but they tried to alleviate her anxiety by saying that her husband would certainly be safe. He had not been brought to this First Aid Post; he must be alright! 'First Aid Post' – a most dreadful euphemism, I soon discovered. As I strolled around looking in the school windows, I remember freezing inside. I saw my first dead body – no, I saw many dead bodies, and parts of dead bodies. No child should ever witness such a spectacle. I became confused. Was it too late to be good in the future? Was God angry with me? I racked my brains to think why. Gradually I reasoned that it was nobody's fault – it was the war.

Eventually, we arrived in Milngavie, sleeping for the night in a Church Hall. For three weeks, my mother searched for my father. We were by this time 'billeted' with a family in Milngavie, and it was here that my maiden aunt and bachelor uncle found us. Their home, in Campbell Street, was burned down. The dreadful news they brought was that my widowed aunt, Mrs Agnes MacIntyre, had been killed in her home in Glasgow Road. (The D.H.S.S. pre-fabricated building was later erected on the site). None of her remains were ever found, in spite of a month's desperate and ferocious digging by her only son. He recovered some crystal beads of his mother's, nothing else. It broke his heart. In the midst of this maelstrom of emotions, we traced my father to the Vale of Leven Hospital. His sister, brother-in-law and their family, my adored 'big' cousins, were all safe in Livingstone Street. (We later discovered that my father had helped to put out fires started when an incendiary bomb exploded in the hospital grounds).

Shortly we moved from Milngavie to Lochgilphead in Argyllshire, mainly because of an aborted bombing raid over Milngavie. My mother and her sister had reached the end of their tether: one dead sister was one too many. My father was transferred to the hospital in Oban, and, with the resilience of the young, I was soon back in the mainstream of community life – school, Sunday school and Brownies. Evacuees we were, but we were good ambassadors for Clydebank. We won practically all the prizes at the local school, no mean feat considering our fractured education since the outbreak of hostilities. I became a 'sixer' in the Brownies and life was sweet again. Every now and again, especially in church, I felt an overwhelming sadness and I wondered where my original classmates had gone. My mind grappled with one piercing truth: life was ephemeral and it was not only old people who died.

After almost two years it was necessary for us to be nearer Clydebank as negotiations were proceeding for us to take up occupancy of a new Burgh house in Durban Avenue, Dalmuir West. We moved to Cumbernauld for fifteen months and my father went to hospital in Millport. In 1944 we moved to Dalmuir and eleven years later to Beech Drive, Parkhall. My father had made a partial recovery but died in 1957 at the age of sixty-two. He had been given only a week to live, the week of the Blitz; when I learned this years afterwards at the time of his death in Blawarthill Hospital, everything fell into place in my mind. My mother's mental anguish at the time of the blitz seemed awesome.

After Dumbarton Academy, Glasgow University and Jordanhill College of Education, I began my teaching career in Linnvale School. I was there on the opening day in 1953 and continued there till my marriage in 1962. My pupils there, thankfully, did not possess all the extended vocabulary of our war-torn childhood. They did not use words like 'direct hit', 'landmine', 'incendiary bomb', nor even 'Blitzkrieg.'

It seems fitting to ask a few questions at this point. From where did 'ordinary,' hard working people find the steely, inward strength, the indomitable spirit and sheer raw courage to overcome such appalling hardships? Did it come from pride? From a sense of community? One thing is certain, the trendiest word of today never crossed their lips: 'counselling'.

John Bowman

A SOLDIER'S HOMECOMING

March 15th 1941. A date I shall always remember. I was granted ten day's leave from my battalion of the Cameronian Regiment, my first leave for five months. I was stationed in a remote village on the east coast of Suffolk.

Hoping to surprise my family by not telling them of my visit, I set off on the long, tedious journey back to Clydebank. A train to Glasgow Central, then a bus for Clydebank at Waterloo Street. When I asked for a ticket to Radnor Street, I was told the bus only went as far as Bon Accord Street, a mile short of my destination. Supposing this to be a wartime restriction, I thought nothing more about it.

When I got off the bus and began to walk along Dumbarton Road, I noticed marks on the buildings which looked like shrapnel holes. To my horror, as I turned into Kilbowie Road, I could see the beginning of the devastation that had been wrought on Clydebank. There was a bomb crater and a piece of tram rail suspended on the overhead tram wires and, further ahead, piles of still smouldering debris of collapsed tenement buildings. Parts of Bannerman Street had gone, but I did notice the building between Bannerman Street and Montrose Street was intact and the Co-op Butcher's shop was open, wide open, as the windows had been blown out. The shop manager, whom I knew, called me in. He told me not to make for the family home in Church Street. It had been demolished by a bomb. He told me my family had all been killed.

Stunned, I hurried away. I was making for Parkhall where I had some friends. En route, I passed Church Street. There was utter dereliction. Where the house had been was a crater and scattered about were the remains of Anderson shelters. As a large family, we were allocated two shelters, which my father had dug into the garden as one long shelter. In Circular Road, I met a lady I knew, and, from her, I got new information. She told me my family had not all been killed. She had seen one of my young sisters leaving the area on a lorry going to Garelochhead. When she heard I had been travelling for twenty four hours, this lady took me in and gave me breakfast. Her advice was not to go to Parkhall, as most people had been evacuated from there. Instead she told me to visit the information centre in a church hall in Kilbowie Road.

There I was given the grim news: my mother, a sister and two brothers were dead; two sisters were in Lennox Castle Hospital; two brothers were in Larbert Hospital near Falkirk. They had no information regarding my father, so they told me that I should go to St James Church Hall, which was being used as a mortuary, because I might be the one who had to identify my dead family.

In the hall, I was shocked and appalled at the sight before me. There were rows and rows of dead bodies, burnt, maimed and disfigured, lying there waiting to be identified. I left the hall unable to recognise anyone. Outside to my huge relief, I met my father. He was limping badly, but he related the story of what had happened on Church Street.

When the air raid siren sounded, my mother and other members of the family were at a social in the church hall opposite the house. Along with a few other friends, they went into the shelter, nine adults and four children. My other sister, on seeing the cramped conditions, went into a neighbour's shelter and thus survived the carnage and escaped to Garelochhead. My other brother, Albert, aged 18, was an A.R.P. warden and was patrolling the street. And my father had moved a few doors along the street to talk to a neighbour when the bomb fell. When the building collapsed, a door lifted and then landed on his foot. He still managed to make for the place where the shelter was. Then he found Albert, lying badly injured, with a heavy piece of concrete on top of him. He tried in vain to lift it, and Albert told him to look after the folk in the shelter. Together with a neighbour, my father spent the night, while the raid continued, digging in the debris, bringing out the casualties. All nine adults were killed and the four children were injured.

My father and I spent the next two nights sleeping alongside a number of other people left homeless until an uncle and aunt returned to their home in Dumbarton Road and invited us to stay with them. It was a welcome change from sleeping in the church hall in Renton.

I spent the remainder of my leave going to funerals of various friends killed in the Blitz and visiting others in different hospitals.

These then are the images and recollections which I have of the aftermath of the Clydebank Blitz, when a long awaited ten days of being with family and friends became the worst ten days of my life.

Stuart McKinlay

HOME GUARD

At eighteen years of age, I was a member of the Home Guard, then known as the L.D.V. (Local Defence Volunteers) and lived in the Admiralty cottages between Alexandria and Balloch. On the second night of the Clydebank Blitz, we were mustered in full marching order, armed with rifle and bayonet and five rounds of ammunition. Our job was to control the refugees streaming out from Clydebank and direct them into schools and other suitable accommodation. For our platoon it was the Christie Park school, then known as the Vale of Leven Academy. My own school in fact. I knew it well.

The people were subdued and well behaved, more stunned I think than anything else. Their eyes gave them away. They had that glazed, inward look that came to be known as bomb-happy.

I was supposed to be on sentry duty, but I spent most of the night crossing the school playground to what was normally the girls' cookery classroom with empty babies' bottles, where people were busy supplying hot milk. I returned them full to grateful mothers with hungry babies and tried to avoid answering questions like: 'Have you seen our Agnes?' from distraught people looking for dear ones who were nowhere to be found.

It was a clear moonlight night. The noise was terrific. Sticks of bombs – you could count the seconds between the explosions, anti-aircraft ack-acks, naval guns on the Firth of Clyde, Bofors, multiple pom-poms; the peculiar unsynchronized sound of the four-engined German bombers, a dull thunder, sweeping from east to west across the night sky; searchlights sweeping, probing vainly, trying to cone them. The oil tanks at Bowling blazing fiercely, black smoke billowing. Some night. Yet for a teenager strangely exciting.

We had to get men wakened in the morning for their work would you believe? Most of them in Clyde shipyards and machine shops. I had to get there myself, to Denny's in Dumbarton. The wheels of industry had to keep turning. In the morning I was asleep standing up, leaning on the radiator in the assembly hall. Some old soldier gave me a nudge.

The streets were littered with the shrapnel from our own anti-aircraft guns. Denny's shipyard had been hit. An unexploded landmine had come through the roof of Denny's canteen and was hanging from the rafters by its parachute. Ships were being lost and ships had to be built.

Fortified with black tea, we just had to get on with it.

Margaret Forrest (née Sinclair)

IS THERE ANYONE IN THERE?

My father, who was Officer-in-charge of the Old Kilpatrick and Bowling Home Guard Units, was out at a regular parade meeting held in the S.M.T. bus garages in Old Kilpatrick. My younger brother, John, aged 12 years, was at his regular Thursday night Boys Brigade meeting held in the Barclay Church hall and afterwards, as usual, at his B.B. friend's house for supper. My mother, my older brother Bill, aged 17 years, and I, aged 16 years were at home.

Bill had had a bath and was in bed just before 9p.m. Minutes later the air-raid siren sounded and heavy gunfire started. Bill got up and quickly dressed and we made for the back door to go to our shelter.

Our house was a bungalow, but had a large head-height basement which had reinforced brick columns. My father thought we might be safer there than in an Anderson shelter in the garden, so part of it was made into a comfortable shelter. We had to go down the back steps of the house to reach the basement door, and, just as we were about to do that, a terrible barrage of gunfire started and Mother felt it wasn't safe to go outside. My father had told us that, if at any time we couldn't make it to the shelter, to get under the dining-room table or under a bed. We quickly decided to go under a back bedroom bed, first me then Mother in the middle, then Bill. We had just been there a short time when we heard some explosions, then a loud whistling noise and a whoosh —— then nothing!

It was 9.20p.m. I came to, hearing mother calling my name. Bill was also awake. It was pitch dark. None of us could move. Mother said the explosions must have caused the ceiling to fall down and the legs of the bed to collapse with the weight. Little did we know then that the whole house was on top of us! Mother said if we all pushed hard together we might be able to move the bed, but it was impossible. We were trapped. Bill then said that he could move his right arm but he couldn't feel anything – there was nothing there! We could hear water gushing but didn't smell gas. We all realised by then that something more serious had happened.

Mother said if we all shouted together someone might hear us. This we did repeatedly but there was no reply. After a time we heard a voice shout, 'Is there anyone in there?' It was Mr. Reid, the Air Raid Warden. When he heard our shouts in reply, he said he'd go and get help. It seemed ages before we heard voices calling to us – the rescue squad had arrived!

The Home Guards had been kept on 'stand by' during the raid. About 2 a.m., there was a lull in the bombing and my father decided that he and some of the men would check out the village and also find out if their families were alright. He found John safe in his friend's air-raid shelter, then made his way home. As he got up the hill, he was aware of several vehicles and an ambulance ahead. Something had happened there he thought. Then he saw that where his home had been was now a pile of rubble.

A bomb had fallen in the back garden. There was a crater thirty feet across and the house had collapsed like a pack of cards. Had we been in the basement or in the garden shelter, we would not have survived.

The rescue squad had been there some time and had managed to get mother out first, then me, and we were being attended by the ambulance men. My father helped to recover Bill who was found lying at the edge of the crater.

It was 2.30 a.m. We had been trapped for five hours. We were first of all taken to the temporary first aid room set up in the Parish Church hall and seen by local doctor, Dr. Anderson. Mother was able to walk and didn't appear to have any serious injuries apart from some lacerations (subsequently severe bruising came up all over her body) so she didn't go to hospital. Bill had back injuries and I had a broken pelvis and internal injuries. We were taken to the emergency wards opened at Robroyston hospital.

After weeks in hospital we were finally reunited with our family who had initially been 'taken in' by friends and had by then found furnished accommodation in Balloch. After about fifteen months a new home was bought in Dumbarton. The house in Old Kilpatrick was rebuilt in 1950/51, but we did not go back there.

My brother and I have suffered over the years with back problems due to our injuries, so the trauma of that fateful night never really goes away. Apart from a few items found later when the house remains were being bulldozed into the crater, and our car, which my father was using that night, we lost everything. But we were alive and we had each other, and that was more important than anything else.

Dumbarton Road looking west. On the left is all that remained of Irene Doherty's tenement home.

Irene O'Donnell (née Doherty)

RUN FASTER, IRENE

I waited patiently for our teacher, Mrs McDade, to say, 'Alright children, put your readers away and go and collect your coats. Now remember, quietly....and no running!'

Little did I know as I ran out the gates of St Stephen's Primary School, that afternoon that I would never set foot inside a Clydebank school again.

As I happily skipped down Duntocher Road past Dalmuir Public School, all I could think of was the picture I was going to see with my father that night. Shirley Temple was undoubtedly every eight year old's favourite child film star, and I was, without any shadow of doubt, her number one fan.

Short interludes, accompanied by music, were not altogether uncommon occurrences in picture halls in those days. However, this time it was no technical hitch within the confines of the projectionist's room.

'AIR RAID IN PROGRESS. PATRONS WISHING TO LEAVE THE CINEMA MAY DO SO AT THEIR OWN RISK'. Those words were projected on to the screen, prior to a few lights being switched on to assist those wishing to leave. There was certainly no panic. As this would no doubt be another one of those false alarms, the majority of patrons chose to remain.

As we made our way to the foyer, I aired my disappointment to my father. 'It'll be just another false alarm,' I moaned.

'I know pet, but we can't take a chance with your granny,' replied my father sympathetically.

My maternal grandmother, a wheel-chair bound invalid, lived with us in our first floor room and kitchen at 835 Dumbarton Road, next to Ross Memorial Church and close to the Dalmuir West tram terminus. She seldom left the house as my mother depended on my father to get her up and down two flights of stairs.

Thinking of my father's understandable concern, I soon calmed down. However, I still found it hard to conceal my disappointment as we were ushered out of the Regal's cosy central-heated atmosphere into the comparative chill of the March night air.

My father had already checked his watch. It was almost 9 p.m. There was not a cloud in the sky as we headed west towards the Forth and Clyde Canal bridge. Indeed, with a full moon that night, it was hard to realise that there was a blackout.

'Stop dawdling, Irene!' said my father as he urged me to quicken my pace. The silent sweeping of the searchlights in the sky fascinated me. I felt no fear or apprehension.

However, those dull thuds we heard after crossing the canal bridge suddenly got louder and louder. My father, now breaking into a run, almost pulled me off my feet as he repeated over and over again, 'Run faster, Irene, run!'

An A.R.P. warden urged us to take cover, but my father was determined to get home. Seeing that I couldn't possibly keep up the pace, he gave me a 'carry-coal bag' over the last few hundred yards. As we reached our close, the noise of exploding bombs was indescribable. For the first time in my life, I experienced a feeling of real fear, a feeling which soon turned to terror. My mother, grandmother and Mrs McArthur, one of our upstairs neighbours, were seated in our hallway when we arrived.

Before long things started to fall from the walls. Dishes smashed as one big bomb rocked the tenement to its foundations. My father decided it was about time we made our way downstairs to the back of the close. He was just about to get some blankets when there was a blinding flash followed by sheer chaos and terror. I found it hard to breathe as our hallway was full of dust and dirt. What made it all the more terrifying was that the blast had blown out all our candles and left us in the dark. My grandmother had serious head injuries, my mother had a broken arm and I had a sore eye. As it was nipping, I thought I had got some dust in it.

It seemed such a long time before we were rescued. A bomb which had penetrated our stairwell had blown most of our landing away. Our rescuers bridged the gap by using our door and doorframe which fortunately had been blown out in the blast. Had it been blown inwards, it would have been worse.

Although I can't recall it, we were apparently given first aid prior to being led on to buses which were lined up along Dumbarton Road. Unfortunately the road behind them had been blocked after the front wall of a tenement had collapsed on to it. So we travelled west to Old Kilpatrick before heading east to Glasgow along the Boulevard. As a good number on our bus were injured, the driver put in at the Western Infirmary before continuing on his way.

I later learned that the damage to my grandmother and myself was caused by flying glass from the internal glass panel door in our hallway. Despite being criss-crossed with sticky tape in the recommended manner it was blown to smithereens in the blast.

The following day the surgeon decided that my eye, which had been penetrated by glass, would have to be removed. My grandmother, whose head was badly injured, was transferred to Killearn Hospital where she remained for several months. My mother's arm was put in plaster and she was allowed to leave the Western the following day with my father. Old friends of hers, District Nurse Kate Curran and her sister Mamie, took us into their home in Uddingston.

As an eight-year-old girl it took me many years to come to terms with having an eye removed. I used to feel very angry about it. I'm sure that many of the personal hang-ups I suffered from during those early years could have been avoided or certainly lessened had I, and many folk like me, been offered some form of counselling, either during or following hospitalisation. But nobody in authority seemed knowledgeable enough to identify and treat the thousands of war-time victims who suffered from post traumatic stress and other psychological problems.

When my family eventually returned to Dalmuir nine years after that terrible night, I didn't recognise the place. Now seventeen years of age, I not only felt a stranger – I was a stranger. Within weeks, I started in Singer as a trainee machine shop inspector. Two years later, I met my husband Neill O'Donnell at the dancing in Dalmuir Masonic Hall, less than a stone's throw from where that dreadful trauma started all those years ago – the Regal Cinema. Neill and I were married three years later and celebrate 46 years of happy married life this year.

Susie McLaughlin (née McCusker)

I'M JOHN McCUSKEY

My late mother had a family of ten – six boys and four girls. When the war came, Peter, who was married, went to the navy. James was a carpenter turned diver. Terry was called up just as he was finished serving his time as an engineer. He was a P.O. in the navy, serving in the minesweepers. Pat the youngest volunteered just after the blitz and my mother was left with one son John, the eldest Andrew having died at six years of age.

It was the thirteenth of March 1941. My sister and her three children were staying with us, having been bombed out of Portsmouth a week previously. On that night, Pat said to me, 'Susie, let's go to the Hibs hall.' This was a place for soldiers who were stationed up the Burn Road. So we went, Pat and his pals and me and Annie and Cathy Toal. No sooner were we in the hall when the sirens went. An army officer was at the door shouting, 'Right, you men are wanted to man the guns!'

So we all had to crawl out that hall and into a close in the Veitches Court. The next thing the airwarden (our uncle Eddie) came along telling us we had to get out of there. It wasn't safe. By this time the bombs were dropping so we were led to a shelter. Davie's yard got it, and the public school. And the close we were in was no longer there. What an escape!

We were in the shelter until the all-clear went and then we all went home. My mother had been frantic wondering what had happened to us. So, the next day she wouldn't let us out of her sight.

It was the fourteenth of March and over the bombers came again. Along with our neighbours, we went to the Anderson shelter in our back garden. My brother John, who was putting out incendiaries, wouldn't come into the shelter. We could hear, 'John, over here! The school's been hit.' It was Father Cassidy and Father McCabe. The two priests were on the other side of the wall which separated our house from St Mary's school.

By this time, the bombers had got St Mary's chapel and the police station. The three men never stopped putting out incendiaries the whole night. As it happened it was my brother John's birthday, and he couldn't help saying, 'Father, the Nazi b....... are bombing my maw's house on my f...... birthday!'

That night passed, and what a sight met our eyes in the morning! There was a large crater in the middle of Auchentoshan Avenue right next to Morrison Street where we lived. Everyone had to be evacuated.

John went down to Bob Dick's pub, bought three bottles of whisky, came back, stood at our gate and gave out drams to every old person in the village.

As I said, we had to be evacuated. John stopped a coal lorry and asked them to take us to Rosyth. We all got into the lorry and John gave the driver a bottle of whisky. On the road to Rosyth, our friends got off at different places: Kirkintilloch, Kilsyth, Stenhousemuir, Denny, Loanhead. My brother Pat had disappeared but we found out that he had gone up the hills with his friend Hughie. My sister and her three children were taken to Bearsden and put into the Archbishop's House.

A week later, I had to come back as I had wages lying in the biscuit factory where I worked. In the factory, I witnessed a young van boy lifting a bomb and being killed. I ran along the Boulevard crying. I came into the village looking for John, who had stayed on to try to put our house to rights. I met a friend who asked me if I was alright. I said, 'No, I've had a shock. 'He got me a cup of tea from the W.V.S. van at the corner and then went into the pub and came out with a brandy and put it into my tea. What a day! When my mother heard that my brother Pat had volunteered for the army, she cried.

Before the war, my brother John had written a song called 'I'm John McCuskey, I like the whisky.' All the village boys used to sing it. Before the war was over it was sung in war zones all over the world.

These are some of my wartime memories and some of my brother John's. It was a war which changed everybody in lots of ways. I wonder will they ever learn.

Kathleen L. Ritchie

CLYDEBANK HIGH CLASSMATES

In March 1941, I was a girl of seventeen. I was brought up on Clydeside. Not, however in Clydebank, but in Dumbarton. Clydebank was to us a place we passed through on our way to Glasgow. Seen from the bus or train, Clydebank meant, for the most part, John Brown's shipyard. There was also Singer's with its huge clock, reputed to be larger than Big Ben, and its vast yard of timber, neatly stacked and set out to season. There was the magnificent hill of tenements, rising one above the other, which was known to us as 'The Holy City' and these and other landmarks were permanent fixtures in our young lives.

After the start of the war we came to know some of the Clydebankers, since pupils from Clydebank High School joined us in Dumbarton Academy. It was some kind of wartime measure, the exact reason for which I have forgotten. I remember we enjoyed sharing classes with these others of the same age and at the same stage of school life. They wore a different uniform and came from a different town and there was a lot of rivalry, but many new friendships were made.

Of course the war was all important. Very soon we, in fifth year, would be leaving school and would be joining up or doing our bit for the war effort in whatever way we could. In the meantime, at the beginning of March 1941 we had our Higher Leaving Certificate exams to sit.

For those of us in school then, our Highers were as important to us as they are to present-day pupils. They were the culmination of years of hard work and for months they had occupied nearly all our waking thoughts. None of us could possibly have believed that, before the last exam (which was Chemistry), all thoughts of Highers would be completely banished from our minds. What happened was the night of March 13th.

I cannot remember at what time the sirens went off that night. My father, who was an air-raid warden, put on his arm band and his tin helmet and went on duty. We did not then have an air-raid shelter in the garden. We, that is, my mother, two brothers and myself, stayed together downstairs in the kitchen and closed the inside shutters on the windows. We settled down with blankets and pillows for what we hoped would be just an hour or two.

Often nothing happened and it would seem to us to have been a false alarm. Sometimes it would be a reconnaissance plane or a lone raider. We had no means of knowing. We simply did as we had been told to do and waited.

As time passed and we listened to that steady continuous menacing throb something was gradually becoming clear to us. Yes, there were bombs, but we were not the target. We had the shipyard and the aircraft factory and Babcock and Wilcox but, whatever was happening out there, we were just on the periphery. What we were experiencing was nothing compared to further up river.

Two or three times during the night we heard the strangely comforting sound of footsteps on our gravel as our air-raid warden came round to check that we were all right.

We were to have other air-raids on other nights. Looking back over all these years, I find I cannot distinguish between them. In the month of May, two months after Clydebank, again on nights of full moon and perfect weather, there was another blitz on Clydeside, in which I believe, Greenock and Port Glasgow suffered most.

I have memories of sitting huddled in an Anderson (or was it Andersen?) shelter with a candle burning under a flower pot to keep us warm, and hearing neighbours in their shelters singing. From time to time we could make out 'Roll out the Barrel'. I remember having a laugh with our visiting warden who told us he could not find anybody in the farm up the road. He had been very worried until he came across the whole family – father, mother and five children – very sensibly, and apparently quite happily, sitting in a row in the ditch with iron pots on their heads.

We learned the different sounds of our local anti-aircraft guns. There were times when we found it exciting seeing the searchlights criss-crossing the sky, sometimes picking out a tiny aeroplane shining silver like a firefly. On one occasion, when we saw a German plane shot down, I remember cheering wildly without sparing a single thought for its occupants. We were, or we thought we were, fighting back.

But my memory of March 1941 is quite different. The blitz on Clydebank was too heavy, deliberate, prolonged, concentrated and remorseless to do other than strike fear, which was the intention.

I do not know at what point during that night we ventured out and saw the flames. The sight of that vast, flaring, noisy sky was beautiful, dramatic and utterly, shockingly horrifying. Some conception of what such a sight meant in terms of death, destruction, pain, suffering, bereavement and loss would gradually be borne in upon us. But not yet. We were witnessing something far too terrible for the human mind to accept.

Morning came eventually and with it the all-clear. Weather-wise it was a perfect spring morning but the sky was covered with a thick pall of heavy, black smoke from burning oil, so that we were in semi-darkness.

We checked round our neighbours. A friend came for me and we went to school. In front of Dumbarton Academy was, or is, a large area of common ground, known simply as the Common and we were amazed to see that this was crowded with people.

As we approached we saw that they were dusty, dirty and dishevelled and many were only in their nightclothes. Some had a few belongings. Many had nothing. They were very quiet, not speaking or crying or complaining. They just seemed stunned. They had come there to the Common from Clydebank, but I'm sure most of them knew not how.

We moved through them to the school which was a hive of activity. We were lent bicycles and sent to a primary school in Vale of Leven which had been organised as one of many rest centres. All day we gave out tea and soup and hot meals which the school-meals service provided. We got the impression that very many people were organising help of every kind but we were much too busy to see anything of the whole picture. In the evening we were sent home to endure another night.

Later, we would hear more and see more and begin to understand more about what had happened in Clydebank. Not, however, from any of our Clydebank High classmates. Weeks later we would perhaps hear of this one living with an aunt in Inverness, or that one in a croft in Skye, but most of us never saw any of them again.

Catherine McIlhenny (née McDermott)

CHURCH HALL IN DOUGLAS STREET

In 1941, I was thirteen. On Thursday 13th March my pal Rita O'Neil invited me and another pal, Cathie Morris, up to her home in Langholm Street, Yoker after school. The O'Neils were on the top flat of the tenement and, when the sirens sounded we all went into the lobby, Mr and Mrs O'Neil, Rita, her sister, Cathie and me. Because it was lasting so long, Mrs O'Neil put us to bed. But we didn't sleep with the noise of the bombs, which was very frightening.

In the morning, Cathie and I made our way home to Union Street. We were shocked at the damaged buildings we saw. My mother and her sister, my Aunt Annie, were in the English Church Hall in Douglas Street, my mother being very relieved to see me.

Aunt Annie had been rescued from her blitzed house in Napier Street. She was pregnant at the time and was holding her youngest child, Evelyn, aged three in her arms. When she was rescued, Evelyn was found to be dead. That night, Aunt Annie lost five children (Mary, 19, Frank, 14, Johnny, 13, Rita,9, and Evelyn,3) and also her husband Frank.

Aunt Annie was caught in the rubble of the burning building. It had her pinned down by the hair and she could not move her head. The firemen were hosing down the building, and water was gradually seeping up to her chin. She was freed just in time. The baby she was expecting was born a few months later, apparently unharmed.

Agnes Watson

CHILD'S EYE VIEW OF WAR

WAR, that stark black word on the orange placard.
How can one word describe the evil to come?
A world of darkness, black windows in the houses and shops,
Baffle walls to impede our progress,
The wail of the siren sending a chill through everyone,
The relief of the All Clear,
The smell of the oil drums providing a smokescreen,
A barrage balloon behind our house,
Lord Haw Haw who got under everyone's skin,
Sitting as quiet as mice while the news was on,
Soldiers from allied countries in different uniforms,
Changing the guard at Buckingham Palace
In battledress instead of colourful tunics,
Women and children queuing for rations and occasional treats,
Fathers working long hours, seeing little of their children,
Adults' serious faces,
Sandbags on landings.
Conductresses calling out bus stops,
Stations and shop fronts devoid of town names,
Weeping women saying goodbye to loved ones at Central Station,
Children with luggage labels round their necks waiting for evacuation,
The horror of the Blitz,
Huddling in closes as the bombs dropped all around us,
Seeing atrocities in the cinema newsreels,
Sights and sounds too horrible to relate.
This is a child's eye view of WAR.

WARTIME FOOD

I believe that everyone was much healthier during the war although we didn't appreciate it at the time. I never remember being hungry as my family could make meals from food that wasn't rationed. Apart from tripe, I enjoyed them all although some didn't sound palatable. For instance, ox hearts were stuffed with breadcrumbs and herbs; we had kidney soup; excellent potted hough was made from ox cheeks; calf tongues were baked and pressed; rabbit stew just like the cowboys; herring (how I hated the bones); mutton pies from the local bakers. A treat was a fish supper – on Saturdays only, as it wasn't considered a meal for a working man.

How I loved it when occasionally tinned fruit appeared in the shops. I welcomed the shortage of eggs, but deplored the disappearance of my favourite fruit, bananas. Canada sent apples to the school which were handed out – one each. We shone the skins up on our jumpers and the insides were pure white. We queued along the school corridors when Rhodesia sent Dairy Milk Chocolate (thirty-two squares) and dates, everyone hoping for the chocolate which wasn't available here, as sweets were zoned and the London area had Dairy Milk Chocolate and we had Milky Ways. I remember going home with the chocolate and being told to share out the thirty-two squares with neighbours and everybody else. I was lucky if I got one myself! That was life then. If somebody needed help to carry their shopping, you were supposed to give it.

When we had school dinners, which were fivepence, I usually got sixpence, which left a penny over. For this amount, two dry rolls could be had or a raw carrot which could be cleaned before eating by scraping it on a pebble-dashed wall. Boys smoked cinnamon stick and chewed away on disgusting licquorice stick which was khaki coloured and stringy.

So you can see that during wartime necessity really was the mother of invention.

SONGS AND ENTERTAINMENT

I wonder if anyone remembers the homemade toys we had during the war when toys were scarce. These were made in local factories: wooden tommy guns; wooden kangaroos which could only work when placed on a board at a slant, triangular kaleidoscopes made with scrap metal and mirrors.

When we stayed at home in the evenings, we listened to the Big Bands – Joe Loss, Eric Winstone, Carroll Gibbons, Ted Heath and Ambrose. When we heard the strains of the orchestra, we knew immediately what band it was and who were the singers.

Then there were radio programmes like, Garrison Theatre, Monday Night at Eight, Paul Temple, I.T.M.A., Dick Barton, Saturday Night Theatre.

Here are some of the many songs that helped us keep our spirits up during those dark and uncertain days:

We're gonna hang out the washing on the Siegfried Line. Have you any dirty washing mother dear?

Run, rabbit, run, rabbit, run, run, run.
Don't give the farmer his fun, fun, fun.

I don't want to set the world on fire,
I just want to start a flame in your heart.

Hey! Little Hen! When, when, when
will you lay me an egg for my tea?

Underneath the lantern by the barrack gate,
Darling I remember the way you used to wait.
My Lilli of the lamp-light, my own **Lilli Marlene**.

There was ham, ham mixed up with the jam in **the quarter master's stores**. My eyes are dim, I cannot see, I have not brought my specs with me (repeat).

Yours till the stars lose their glory. Yours till the birds fail to sing.

Bless 'em all, bless 'em all! The long and the short and the tall;
Bless all the sergeants and double-U-O ones,
Bless all the corp'rals and their blinkin' sons....

We'll meet again don't know where, don't know when.

But I know we'll meet again some sunny day.

Roll out the barrel, we'll have a barrel of fun.
Roll out the barrel, we've got the blues on the run.

That certain night, the night we met, there was magic abroad in the air.
There were angels dining at the Ritz,
and **a nightingale sang in Berkley Square**.

Mares eat oats and does eat oats – Oh!
Mairzy doats and dozy doats and liddle lamzy divey.
A kiddley divey too, wouldn't you-oo?

I'll be seeing you in all the old familiar places.
That my heart and mind embraces all day through.

Kiss me goodnight Sergeant-Major. Tuck me in my little wooden bed.
We all love you, Sergeant-Major when we hear you bawling 'Show a leg!'

There'll be Blue Birds over **The White Cliffs of Dover**,
Tomorrow just you wait and see.

You are my sunshine, my only sunshine,
You make me happy when skies are grey.

I've got sixpence, jolly jolly sixpence,
I've got sixpence to last me all my life.

MARCH 13, 1941

As I fumbled sleepily with my clothes taking them off as they were being put on, there seemed to be a lot of to-ing and fro-ing. 'Quick, quick wake up. The siren's gone, we've got to get down to the close.' There were five people in the house at the time, including myself. We hurried downstairs with the neighbours to the close, which was strengthened with steel poles and cross struts.

We had suitcases which were always packed ready to take with us. Our friends in Liverpool had been bombed out previously and only had the clothes they stood up in, so they warned us to be ready.

My father had been attending a meeting in the Burgh Band Hall and had hurried home when he saw by the burning wood pile in Singer's that it was not a false alarm. He had his heavy navy blue overcoat on and he opened it and I stood inside hugging him. Others were standing around and some sat on suitcases. The people who lived in the close lay on a quilt in the lobby with the door open.

I remember thinking if the building should get hit I hoped it would be an incendiary bomb as I thought it would give us time to get out.

When we got back into the house, my bed was ruined with shards of glass from the window, although we had had it taped as ordered. Later, when looking through the front room window (minus the glass) I saw lots of people walking towards Clydebank and some women were carrying bundles on their backs and I wondered where all the 'rag wives' were coming from. Apparently they were homeless people walking to the Union Church nearby which was a gathering point.

Later that day we all went to an open lorry that had been commandeered by either the army or the Home Guard and sat against our suitcases. We went to stay for a short while with relatives in Glasgow. In the May, I was sent to friends in Annan in the Borders and, when I asked how long I would be staying, I was always told: 'for the duration.'

V.E. DAY AND ON

As the war in Europe was drawing to a close, everyone hugged the radio for news of the surrender. I remember sitting in my pyjamas ready for bed when the news came through. I got dressed and joined everyone who was flooding on to the streets. We milled about wondering where to go and what to do. First of all we walked to Dalmuir Park which was crowded and eventually, when nothing was happening, we all trooped up to the Town Hall. Some people were saying, 'The Provost and the Councillors should be here,' and others, 'Where's the Burgh Band?' This annoyed my father

Agnes Watson with her father, Tommy Gardiner, in Burgh Band uniform, and her mother, Agnes Gardiner.

who proceeded to explain why the band wasn't there. However, everyone just wandered aimlessly along talking non-stop and feeling really happy, and then after a few hours, we all went home again.

Parties were laid on for the children and women machined wallpaper into party hats and there was food and party games. The money for this was collected round the doors. One of the parties was in the backcourt, and Dick English and friends carried a piano downstairs so that we could have music. We also had a party in the Dalmuir Former Pupils Hall.

Later on, closes were decorated with flags and bunting and 'Welcome Home Joe' or whatever the name was, for the returning members of the forces and again parties were held.

Church bells could be pealed again – they were silent during the war because they were to be a sign of invasion. Blackout curtains came down and house and shop lights shone out and when evening came, we would stand at our window and try to count all the lights. We went into town to see the neon lights on the buildings – a particular favourite was the 'Ba Bru' sign which could be seen from the top of Renfield Street.

I really can't describe the feeling I had, but I had the same feeling again when I saw the Berlin Wall come down.

James McBride

A PLACE CALLED CLYDEBANK

I well remember the sirens going on the 13th March 1941. I lived with my mother, father, brothers and sisters at 9 Kilmun Lane, Maryhill, Glasgow. My Dad had been called up and had joined the R.A.F. several weeks previously.

When the warning sounded, our family all went downstairs into the house of Mr and Mrs Hamilton, who were friends of ours and lived in the close. After a while we heard the explosions and guns going off in the distance. This went on for hours, and we talked a lot and played games to pass the time. I don't recall being frightened in any way. At last the all-clear sounded and we trooped back upstairs and into bed.

In the morning we heard of the terrible things that had happened in a place called Clydebank. I'd never heard of this place before and, in those days, it was a long way away.

That night, the 14th of March, the sirens went again. As before, we all went downstairs into the close and our friends' house.

What happened to us a while later is branded into my mind and will remain there until the day I die.

I see the picture of where everyone was. It's as if the moments are frozen in time. If you can visualise a single end with the usual hole in the wall bed. A deal table and chairs scrubbed almost white. There was an armchair either side of the fireplace. My mum was sitting next to me in the armchair. I was sitting on the fender in front of the fire with my back against the gas cooker. Mrs Hamilton was in the other armchair nursing baby Charlie. Margaret, my sister, was on a stool between us. My brother Billy was at the end of the table with Mr Hamilton, and my sisters, Sadie and Grace were playing some kind of game.

Suddenly there was a whistling noise in my ears, then choking dust and darkness except for a tiny glow from the remains of the fire.

I shouted and screamed for my mammy, shouted for everybody by name but no-one answered. After a while I heard groaning and when I called out again, Margaret answered. She was buried and in great pain. We screamed and shouted and the Hamiltons' dog barked and barked adding to the noise.

I must have passed out, because the next thing I remember, I was in an ambulance, wrapped up in a blanket and sitting on someone's knee. I remember I had no trousers on. What happened to them I don't know, anyway I didn't care. I was taken to a casualty clearing station. I remember being given very sweet tea and being very, very sick. I was then taken to a hospital, and, the following day, I was again taken by ambulance to another hospital, quite a long journey away, the Law hospital in Carluke. I knew nothing of what had happened to any of my family or what was going on.

It was two weeks later before my father came for me. Until then he didn't even know I was alive. He thought we had all died that night. Someone visiting the hospital had recognised me and passed the information to him.

I remember I was playing on the balcony outside the ward and, seeing someone in an airforce uniform, somehow I knew it was my dad. I rushed to him and threw myself into his arms. We both cried and cried. He didn't need to tell me. I knew my family were all dead.

My grandfather, grandmother and uncles stayed in Kilmun Street across the backcourt from us. Grandad McBride, Cousin Bertie McBride and Uncle James Buick, who was home on leave from the forces, were all killed that same night. My grandmother survived. She and I went to Ireland and stayed there out of harm's way for two years.

A. M.

REQUESTING AN AMBULANCE

At the time of the Blitz, my husband was very ill. With our daughters Chrissie, aged six and Ina aged eight, we were living in Whin Street where we had been for just three weeks.

On that day, I had taken the girls to town for raincoats, for going back to Radnor Park School. At home that night, after tea, the girls went to bed, and then the sirens started. At first nobody paid much attention. Then we heard the bombs falling on the oil tanks at Old Kilpatrick.

I went into the bedroom where the girls were sleeping and found that one of the chairs had been set alight by an incendiary bomb! Then the outside door of our four-in-a-block house blew in and cut my leg. The incendiaries were dropping all around, a scene from a terrible fairyland. Water was gushing down the street.

I sent the girls off, running down, shouting and screaming, into the shelter. My husband was so ill that he didn't want to move, but I managed to get us all to the shelter. There we sat all night, listening to the bombs falling. It was bitter cold, and our feet were in the water that came up quite a few inches in the shelter.

The next morning we were all like sweeps coming out of the shelter. Our roof and our living room wall were down. We couldn't get into the house, so I set off to look for a cup of tea. Chrissie and Ina went down to Janetta Street School and, through the window, they saw dead bodies. Then a man came and hunted them.

On the Friday morning, my husband's two brothers arrived and took the girls away to Renton, leaving me on my own to work with my ill husband. He needed to be in a hospital, so I walked away down to the Town Hall and requested an ambulance. None arrived, so at eight o'clock that night I put him back into the shelter. I remember him wearing his pyjamas, socks and slippers and a pixie-hood knitted at the school by Chrissie. The sirens went again, and, that second night, I remember landmines, falling by parachute and making huge craters. I thought we'd never survive.

In the morning, after settling my husband, still in his pyjamas and pixie, in the garden, I set off again to look for transport. I caught sight of a doctor getting into his car and asked him if he would take my husband down to the Town Hall. But he refused, saying he had to get over to Bearsden to see his family.

I was desperate by this time. Then I caught sight of a pram, and I asked a policeman if I could take it, explaining what it was for. He said, 'Oh my, that's terrible! Aye, just take it.'

When I got back, two men, neighbours, helped me to get my husband into the pram. I set off pushing him and, when I got to the top of the hill, there were a whole lot of people waiting for buses to take them away from the town. My husband was well known in Clydebank –he had his own band- and I felt so embarrassed for him. I was even more embarrassed when a wheel came off the pram! Finally I got him down to the Town Hall, and demanded that he get the necessary hospital treatment. Then I left him and went to see if my mother, who lived in Cunard Street, was alright. Her house had suffered just one broken pane of glass.

That morning, walking with her towards Renton, we got the length of somewhere about Bowling, where a lovely couple took us in and the woman gave us a lovely cooked breakfast. But I felt too grimy to stay and go into the nice bed.

When I got the girls again, I took them and my mother to a Masonic Hall in Alexandria, and we slept there two or three nights, waiting to be billeted. My sister Jean came down one day and took us into a café in Alexandria for a meal. The girls thought this was a great treat – Paris buns and greengage jam!

Then, one by one, the families all got housed. In the mornings, a soldier used to shout out to waken the men to go to work. 'Six o'clock and all's well!' he used to shout. I was so fed up with this at six a.m. that I remember saying, 'If he shouts that again, I'll shout six o'clock and go tae hell!' We were the last family to be housed. It was eerie in that big hall all by ourselves.

Helen McNeill

MY SPECIAL MUM 'ORPHANED' AGAIN

I lived at 11 Burns Street, the home where I was born and I had a happy carefree childhood with my sister, brother and friends from school. Although we were told about the war and had heard the siren on several occasions, we did not realise the seriousness of the situation – we were more excited about being issued with gas masks which we felt very proud to wear over our shoulder. We also had mock air raid practice at school to evacuate from the classroom to the air raid shelter.

At home, when we went to bed, all our clothes were close by, coats, hats and shoes, in the event of a raid during the night. Beside our clothes was my mother's 'policy bag' in which she kept all the insurance policies, birth certificates and so on, and these went with her everywhere she went.

The 13th March started off differently for us, as my mother had told us there was a Shirley Temple film on at the Regal Picture House and she and my father were taking us there that night. As we normally only got to the matinee to see films, it was a rare treat to get out after tea and we were all very excited.

My mother was orphaned early on in her life and had been brought up by two uncles and her grandfather, now deceased. We as children spent many times in their house, as they were like grandparents to us, so on that evening we all went in to see them to tell them we were going to the pictures. Sometimes my brother would stay overnight in their house and it was discussed that perhaps he would stay that night instead of going to the pictures. But it was decided he would go to see the film and we would take him back to the uncles' house in Pattison Street on the way home.

The five of us took off on our outing, getting on the tramcar at the bottom of Pattison Street and getting off at the Regal Picture House, a very short journey but it added to the excitement of the evening as we did not travel by tram very often.

We went into the picture house and saw the shorter film and the news and were well into the screening of the big film when the siren sounded. At that point, a lot of people went to get home. Some, including my father, who were on night firewatch, had to go out. But mainly we were advised that everyone who could stay would be safer until the all-clear sounded.

For a short time the film continued and then it was stopped. Just imagine how we children felt at having our Shirley Temple taken from us. That was a real tragedy. However, people began to get up on to the platform and sing and we all joined in. I think the reason the community singing was encouraged was to help drown out the noise of the planes. But suddenly an incendiary bomb came through the roof and landed on the stage. The wardens ran on with pumps and water hoses and everyone in the hall was moved to the back underneath the balcony. That put paid to the singers who were a bit worn out by this time.

As the night wore on we could hear all sorts of bombs falling and planes flying low. It was quite frightening but there was a great sense of security as the adults were keeping us all reassured. Every so often someone would shout in that such and such an area had 'got it!' and I kept hoping my dad would come back. My mother took me out to the toilet and, although the window pane had been blacked out, some of the paint was scraped from the window (with something like 'Jimmy loves Mary' as I remember) and I could see the huge fire outside. This was the woodpile in Singer's yard which had been hit. That was my very first sight of what was happening outside, but the noise continued into the early hours of the morning.

It was early next morning when the all-clear went and we were allowed out of the picture house and made our way home. No tram journey home this time. The sight that met our eyes was hard to believe. The pavements and road were either covered in debris from the tenements that were halved in two or they were covered in thousands of hoses as firemen and air raid wardens were struggling to put out massive fires. The tram cars were totally damaged and the tram lines were curled up in the air.

As we got to the other side of the road, we passed a pend. I looked in and told my mum that a lot of people in there were sleeping as I saw rows of legs sticking out from the tarpaulins. I was to know at a later date that they were some of the many people who had lost their lives during that terrible night.

My mother was hurrying me along that road to get to her uncles' house. All night she had been saying, 'I hope they are all right.' As we got nearer to our destination, my mother could see her church had been flattened and she got a bit upset at that. We hurried on a bit quicker as the nearer we got to the area of her family home the more we saw buildings down, huge holes in the road and blazing fires everywhere. As we turned the corner into Pattison Street, we saw the uncles' close – just a pile of blazing rubble! My mother ran up to an air raid warden and he just said to her, 'Nobody got out of there, hen!' That night was to change our lives forever.

At that time my mother went away, and it wasn't till later on I realised that she had gone to look for her sister and her sister's family who stayed in Livingstone Street in Clydebank. When she got there, the only part of the street that had been bombed was where her sister's home was, and nobody could tell her anything about the people who had been there. So she was more or less left in exactly the same situation as she had been earlier on that morning when her family home in Dalmuir had been bombed.

At the end of that day we were evacuated to Helensburgh. Every morning Mum would walk us to Clyde Street School. She had made arrangements with a local restaurant to give us lunch. She would then take the bus to Clydebank and there she would stand outside John Brown's yard where her sister's husband worked. Her thoughts at that time were that he might have been at work during the bombing and he might have escaped.

So she stood there every day, watching them all going out, and waiting till they all went back. That went on for three weeks, and then one day, she saw my uncle coming out of the gate. She ran towards him, and he just turned and they both hugged each other and she said, 'Where are you? Where's the family?' And he said the same to her. ' Oh you're alive! You're alive!'

He and his wife knew the uncles were dead because the first thing they did was to go down to the uncles' house and my mother's house as well. The uncles had been killed, so they assumed that my mother and father and the three of us had been in my uncles' house. If we hadn't been at the pictures, we probably would have been there because people tended to go into the bottom houses in the close, these always being the safest.

So obviously they thought that we had all gone over to my uncles' house because it would have been safe. It was a big mix-up. They had then gone to Duntocher to stay with my mother's sister-in-law. And there they were all safe, thinking that our family were dead, while we were all safe in Helensburgh, thinking they were dead.

Fay Kennedy (née Scott)

SECOND EVACUATION

During the 'phoney war' lots of children were evacuated from the towns into the countryside for their safety. For some children, this was a happy experience, for others it was not.

My sister, Elsa, who was nine years old, and I were evacuated and, because I was five years old, I was deemed old enough to go away from home without my mother, and therefore Elsa had the task of looking after me while we were staying with strangers. We were evacuated to Innellan along the Clyde coast which I can see now is a beautiful place, but as a child, away from home, I simply hated it and being separated from my mum and dad.

We travelled from Dalmuir Station to Wemyss Bay by train and then by a Clyde Steamer to Innellan. I was crying when I left my mother but was kindly befriended by a schoolteacher who was accompanying us on the journey and she helped me a great deal during the early days of the four months we were away. After many entreaties, but with some trepidation, my parents brought us home to Dalmuir.

Some eighteen months later, I was evacuated yet again, but this time there was no alternative and I was with both my sister and my mother so I did not mind going, and, in any case, our home had been rendered uninhabitable during the Clydebank Blitz.

When the siren sounded and even when some bombs began to fall, people did not immediately make for the shelters but it became apparent we should seek the safety they afforded. I can remember running from tree to tree shielded by my father. The whole town was ablaze and people were panicking as they searched for their loved ones from whom they had become separated or who had been away from home when the air-raid had begun. It was a very frightening situation but I was young enough to feel safe simply because I was with my father.

When we returned home after the first night, our house was not too bad and my mother and sister began to clear all the plaster and glass off the beds, furniture and carpets. I was allowed to go outside although abjured not to go near any buildings, and I went with a friend to look at all the dead bodies which were laid out on the ground in lines, waiting for their relatives to identify them and claim them.

After the second night of intensive bombing, it was obvious that we had to leave our home. All the ceilings were down, the windows broken with shards of glass hanging on the protective tapes and the doors were hanging off their hinges. Plus, there was a fire in the roof from an incendiary bomb.

We packed a few belongings and my father took my mother, sister and me to join a long, long queue of people and we were eventually driven away on a bus to an unknown destination. We finally arrived in Linwood, which was at that time a very small village, in Renfrewshire. We stayed there for four years, but my father did not join us because, after the Blitz, he lived in the factory where he worked and was very soon called up to serve in the Royal Artillery, which he did for four years.

Having lived through the evacuation, Blitz and war affects you for the rest of your life, but not necessarily adversely. I did not keep any mementoes of the war, perhaps I should have. I could have kept my gas mask (never used), my ration book (always used) or my identity bracelet, worn like a watch on my wrist, kept on day and night and bearing my National Registration Number SJCO 48/4. Somehow or other these things did not seem important and I don't even know what happened to them. All I have are memories and a few photographs which are important to me.

J. Alistair Robertson

SO MUCH FOR GOVERNMENT STATISTICS

Born at 96 Radnor Street, I had moved out to the small village of Condorrat near what is now Cumbernauld New Town prior to the Blitz. But my family still stayed at 100 Radnor Street and on the day of the Blitz my brother Harvey, after his return from work at Babcock's in Renfrew, for reasons known only to himself, went upstairs and filled the bath with water and left a pail beside it. Around 2 a.m., with the raid at its height, he found it almost impossible to light a fag in the communal shelter just across the road, due to the lack of oxygen. So he came out into the bomber's moon, went across into his house and found an incendiary in the process of setting the bathroom door alight. Instinct? I wonder.

My wife's uncle, Edward Donaldson, was one of the few Air Raid Wardens killed in the raid and our local police sergeant at Condorrat, who had spent the night in Clydebank, was able to tell us some weeks later that he and other helpers were just too late to save him from suffocation, and he was buried in a communal grave apparently as unknown. Yet, three weeks later my father-in-law and I were asked to go to Elgin Street School to identify a body as being Edward Donaldson. The body we saw was faceless, but we were assured it was he, and his identity card, gas mask, steel helmet, etc. were there to prove it. And yet, the police sergeant told us that the Edward Donaldson they had tried to save was totally unmarked. 'Our' Edward Donaldson was buried next day in a communal grave at Dalnottar Cemetery. So much for the government statistics re the number killed.

Christina Brown

NOTHING BUT WHAT WE STOOD IN

On March 13th 1941 it was a clear, frosty night with a star-studded sky. I decided to visit friends on Kilbowie hill. I left my brother in our cosy two apartment tenement. At 9 p.m. the air raid sirens blared and about thirty of us crowded into an underground cellar.

The deafening roar of the German Luftwaffe bombers rained death and destruction on our beloved town for eight hours of unrefined hell. At dawn we emerged to a scene of utter devastation forever imprinted in my memory.

I met my brother halfway, at the blazing Singer factory. We hugged each other, so glad we were both alive, and then he prepared me for the shock of seeing the house we were born in being hosed with water from the adjoining canal by airwardens. We had nothing but what we stood in. In a state of shock, we wandered, not knowing where we would lay our heads on that second night of the Blitz. Eventually we were herded on to buses and taken to St Rollox school in Renton where we were given mugs of tea and hot soup and army blankets.

The bombers came over again, their aim being to destroy the Clydeside shipyards. After that we were evacuated for nine months and gave thanks to the Dumbarton people who gave us hospitality and shelter. I learnt the truth of the saying, 'if your name is on it.' I am now 82 years of age, but I could never agree with Noel Coward in his heyday, who sang, 'Don't let's be beastly to the Germans!'

Helen Robertson

AIR-RAID WARDEN

We were part of a section of the air-raid wardens who were based in the hall in Radnor Park church. I was a full time warden at two pound a week, but after a year or two, at the time of the Phoney War, I was paid off and there were just a few full-time wardens kept on. But I remained a part-time warden.

The night of the Blitz I heard it on the wireless at nine o'clock, and I opened the budgie cage and I shut up my fire because I thought if there was a blast it would save the fire being blown out into the house and creating a big fire. Then I went down with my tin hat on and got my neighbours into the shelter in the back court at Second Avenue, bordering on Singer's sports field. Before that every few weeks we used to take turns at visiting the shelters, because they were pretty damp. What you did was you put a candle in a flower pot and then put another flower pot on top, and that took the chill off the air, so that if the shelter had to be used at least it wouldn't be running damp. So with my neighbours we got down into the shelter. We weren't long there till I heard Wheeeeeeee! and I remember very calmly just thinking to myself that was probably the last sound that I'll ever hear. However, the bomb exploded, and even though my eyes were shut, I still saw the flash and suddenly, my mouth was filled with dust. I ran out the shelter and saw the neighbours further up the street running into what I could just describe as a big cloud of dust, for the building had been struck with the bomb that I had heard and I remember shouting, 'Stay where you are! The shelter held!'

I ran through our close and round to the front and there was just a heap of rubble in the street. But people emerged and I remember saying, 'Anybody that's able to walk come with me.' The fact that you had a tin hat on people seemed to think you were immune. However I took these people and put them in the shelter in St Stephen's school and I said to them,

'Now I'll need to go up to Boquhanran school to get an ambulance and if anybody is able to walk come with me.' Two wee girls set off with me up Albert Road and I remember incendiaries were falling just like flowers on a carpet, hundreds of them, and it was no use trying to put them out, at least if they burned out on the street they were doing no harm. Whenever we heard a bomb coming down we would take shelter together.

Just before we got into Boquhanran School, a man appeared with a rifle on his shoulder, and a greatcoat (it was March remember, a cold night) and he said, 'Can I help you?' Now we had been told that if the Germans came they wouldn't be dressed in a Nazi uniform. They would be in disguise. So I waited till this man spoke before I answered, and I said I have these wee girls and we're trying to get into the school. So he helped me and we got them into the school. We just got in and the woman that was there says, 'Have you got the form filled up?' Now we were issued with forms that you put the name and address of any casualties on, and I remember saying to her, 'Nelly, nobody's gonny have had time to fill up any forms. It's just like Hell out there!' They knew nothing because they were in the sanctuary of the school.

I left the wee girls and came out, and told the ambulance to get down to the end of Second Avenue because I knew there must be some people seriously hurt. I had just got out at the school and quicker than I can tell you, the whole roof was just one blaze. There were two or three landmines floating down, though to me a landmine was a big round thing, but these weren't; these were big, long cylinders calmly floating down, slowly, beautiful in the bright, moonlight night. So I got to the junction of Boquhanran Road and Albert Road, and Bill Girvan was there with an auxiliary fire appliance. I said, 'Bill, get up to the school as quick as you can for that roof's on fire.' And he says, 'Ellen, I can't move. I have no water.'

So back down I went and it was chaos. Two closes were flattened. Luckily the ambulance was there before me, and a Mr Malcolm was standing in the ambulance with blood on his head. I said, 'You come out of there,' (a tin hat made you a heid yin), 'you're able to walk.'

And he said quite calmly, 'It's my wee boy. I'm just helping him into the ambulance.' I lifted the end of the stretcher. I had the feeling the wee boy was dead, but I said where he was going they knew better how to deal with him than I did. So I helped him into the ambulance. It was a good job I had got that ambulance down because incendiaries fell in the school playground and burned out all but two ambulances.

However I got back down to my place. The minister, Mr Philp, stayed in Boquhanran Church Manse near the foot of Albert Road and I knew he was often very late at night and his wife could be a wee bit nervous and I thought about her being in that big house herself (although he had been a miner and he had shored up below their stairs and it would have held up to anything except a direct hit). So I went to see if Mrs Philp was alright and just as I got to the gate, him and her came out the house, and I asked them where they were going . He said, 'Oh we don't know, but we just feel it's not very safe.' So I took them through our close which was still standing and put them in our shelter. During this, of course, it was very noisy, with the roar of the flame and the incessant drone of low flying planes. One plane, I remember seeing it as plain as anything, was actually below the level of the flames. There was a number nine bus at the terminus at our close and that plane machine-gunned that bus. There was a high wall between us and Albert Road houses and we could see, right along the length of the wall, machine-gun bullets.

The night went on and there wasn't very much you could do. Periodically I went out and had a look but there just was nothing anybody could do. So I was in the shelter with everybody else.

The next day it was devastation – a bomb had hit the gable-end of our house in Second Avenue and it took away half of that close. Our close was intact but in the two bottom flats, the contents had fallen into a space below- which was the support of the close. I remember we had coal cellars on the stairs and they were all burst open and I remember crawling up over all the coal to get up to my house. The door had burst open and the front of the house was out, but I crawled on my stomach. The wardrobe and sideboard and that had been burst open, so I lay on my stomach and any clothes that I could reach with my hand I threw them out the window. I knew at least they could be cleaned. And, I even threw out a brush and comb, anything I could get my hands on. My very treasured embroidery got thrown out the window and on to the street. When I got down there, I collected up some of the clothes and I put them in what had been just a wee shelter in the street.

Now by this time, dawn had come and I remember St Stephen's Church going up in flames and this woman saying to me, 'Oh that's the end of St Stephen's!' But I just thought to myself there'll be another St Stephen's when there's no more Hitler! So by this time it was light and we were kind of gathering ourselves. Across the road there was the Cooperative grocery. Now things were very scarce at that time – you got your quarter of margarine and your quarter of butter. Anyway, I went across the street and this man, the grocer, was in the Cooperative with his tin hat on. He was only allowing two people in at a time because above them the roof was just in danger of falling down. And wonder of wonders, you could even buy a pound of butter. You could buy tins of jam. Things we never knew existed, things that were kept below the counter. There were no limits.

It was a good job he got rid of that lot because before nightfall that roof did fall in. Next door to that was a wee kind of sweetie shop. Mr Anderson was killed in that shop. Now I don't know who lifted those bodies but on this bit of wall across from our close there were three bodies lying on the street. Somebody had put them there. I presume it was the ambulance men. Each of them was covered with a grey blanket. Our pavement was full of rubble, so you had to walk past these bodies and I'll always remember, one of them: there was a bare leg out of the blanket, I don't know whether of a man or a woman. These bodies lay there for a couple of days.

Now there wasn't any water, so my husband and Mr Hackett that was a neighbour went away looking with kettles. They went away round by the chapel and they found water running down the street. They managed to fill the two kettles. The danger was the clean water and the sewage was all mixed up in below the streets. And when they came back with this precious water, we started to boil it and then it just dawned on us the lavatory cisterns were all full. Now they were all iron, so there was always a thick covering of rust, but we boiled it anyway, and I don't know that anybody ever suffered from it. So we had tea along with the driver and the conductor of the bus that had been bombed.

It was difficult to actually walk on the streets because you were walking on three or four layers of glass. It was like walking on ice. It was just as well that Mr and Mrs Philp were actually in our shelter because theirs had been hit by a landmine. That must have been what tore the front of our building away. It was a flat roof and that had fallen down on what had been my house, the top floor flat.

After that I went away looking for my husband who had been on duty in Radnor Street and I met him coming down looking for me. So at least we were both alive.

Nettie Paterson

ESSENTIALS

The first morning my mother-in-law's windows were blown in. We said to her, 'Pick up your essentials, as we have to go.' She dusted the piano and lifted 'The People's Friend', her hot water bottle and her alarm clock. Next night the building was destroyed. We had a laugh afterwards about it.

Greta Bailey

STOCKING SEAMS

I stayed in Second Terrace and went to Boquhanran School. That was one word I always could spell – Boquhanran. I liked school. Miss Peacock was my beginner teacher and I remember Miss Hogg, who was a musician.

Mr Rossi had an ice-cream parlour, where I used to buy a penny cone. You could get toffee balls and soda lunches from Mrs Morrison's shop in First Terrace, and Mr Russell, the grocer, sold my favourite, Aytoun Sandwich biscuit.

When I left school at the age of thirteen, I worked in Castlebank Laundry in Anniesland. I had to get the 6 a.m. car from Clydebank. Later, I worked in the bottle factory in Halley Street, Yoker, and then Singer's.

I remember we used to sew seams up the back of our stockings, or draw seams on our tanned legs.

Margaret McDermid

SEWING MACHINES TO MUNITIONS

At the time of the Blitz I stayed in Second Avenue and worked in Singer, 43 department. On the night of the thirteenth of March I was working late. We walked home via Dalmuir Gate entrance. One thing I've always remembered was the beautiful moon – it was so bright. As we made our way out, we had to pass many fires. They seemed to form a ring and we were worried about getting through them to reach home.

Grandad, who was in his eighties, lived with us, and we did not want to trail him to our nearest shelter at the corner of Boquhanran Road. However, we eventually had to go. The next morning we found our home destroyed. I remember seeing the oven door, which had been blown off, but still hanging there was the set of tongs. We were left with only the clothes we stood in.

My mother had a sister who lived in Hamilton and that's where we made for. My cousin was able to give me some clothes, which was a blessing. I travelled daily from Hamilton to Clydebank for work. Departments which at one time had made sewing machine parts quickly changed over to munitions.

Sam Black

A DECISION THAT SAVED OUR LIVES

Although the main threads of this story were told to me in later years, four events will remain implanted in my mind forever more. On Thursday 13th March, I was but a few days short of my fifth birthday, and Mr Hitler was about to send me an early, unrequested parcel. The Blacks lived at 43 Livingstone Street on the second floor, one up. The sirens apparently went off about 9 p.m. and I recall like yesterday my dad carrying me down the stairs towards the first landing, as the stained-glass landing window began to shatter due to the exploding bombs. It seemed like daylight outside, and glass was flying everywhere. My mother and seven year old brother Bill must have been behind us. At the ground floor level, for some reason, perhaps it being the nearest door, my dad chose to turn left into the home of the people on the ground floor. That decision may have saved our lives.

The second vivid event was when I was sitting on a mattress beside Bill and between our mum and dad in this narrow lobby, from where I could just see through the window of a front room outside to the street, where a great mass of sparks was making the night into day. The German fliers were dropping landmines by small parachutes and one landed in the street directly in front of our building.

The shelter where the family should have been was situated on the central reservation in the centre of the street and it received a direct hit from a large bomb. The bomb damage left it looking like an elongated M. It also caused the facade of the tenement building to collapse into the street. One of our neighbours in the next close was killed sitting in his armchair and could be seen the next morning when we emerged from the shelter of the ground floor flat. He was one of the air-raid wardens and died during his break from duty.

Our uncles, George and Sam Porter, were not so fortunate. They died along with fifteen others who sheltered in their ground floor flat in Pattison Street, Dalmuir. The building received a direct hit. My brother

Bill apparently should have been staying with the 'uncles' but had not been allowed to go because he had a cold.

The next morning we went out to find the whole front wall of our building collapsed into the street, leaving the apartments exposed like a giant doll's house and I can still see, and will never forget seeing, our furniture hanging and swinging at odd angles from the ceiling of our home. My mother stood and wept at the sight of it all. Had we gone to the right side door the previous night, we surely would have been crushed to death. My dad told us years later that he only had five shillings in his pocket and the clothes he was wearing at the time. He had to go down to Clydebank Library to get some money. I believe they gave him twenty-eight shillings.

Gavin Laird

WALKING INTO BAFFLE WALLS

I never felt lonely in Clydebank. It was a busy town, a bright town, especially on a Saturday. Lots and lots of people, lots and lots of movement, character and life. Unlike just now. Sadly it's a bit of a mess now, not like it used to be. There were thousands of men from the shipyard rushing out of the gates, and the gates so narrow! I've witnessed tramcars waving about with the pressure of all these guys wanting to get home, who could blame them, as they all tried to get on the first tram.

At school we were given siren drill. And one thing that happened: they built these dreadful baffle walls outside the closes and with it being so dark, many a sore nose people got, including myself, because (think about it) there was no street lighting at all and in the middle of the pavement at the close entrance a brick wall! People used to walk into them.

In terms of the population as a whole being drilled for the eventuality of an air-raid, that was non-existent. Of course, when the bombing did take place, to some extent, perhaps we suffered the consequences of that.

On the night of 13th March, I went to the pictures, to a picture hall that no longer exists in Clydebank, the Palace, along with two of my mates, the two Doyle lads. During the night, as the time went on, there was a lull in the bombing and Nicky, Eddie and I got off our marks and shot past the man at the door and ran like hell up Kilbowie Road. We were about halfway up the hill when the incendiaries began to come down. It was like looking at falling flames or rain that was on fire raining down on Clydebank and the graveyard. And if you were an eight year old, it was like some kind of horror film.

The father of Nicky and Eddie Doyle, his name was Eddie, in the middle of the bombing had left the shelter where my mother and the rest of his family were sheltering, to look for his two boys and Joe Soap here. He eventually found us, quite incredible, you would need to have a vivid imagination to be able to describe it, because there was an awful lot of bombs falling and buildings were on fire.

We managed to get to our house in Third Terrace and were allowed a brief period of time to grab one or two bits and pieces. By this time, it was the next day, my eighth birthday, and my mother had bought me a brand new pair of football boots. But instead of grabbing my football boots, I grabbed my schoolbag. We were dispersed and we ended up in Kirkintilloch. Not that we were welcomed except in the miners' quarters. The other parts of the town, particularly the well off parts didn't welcome these refugees. We got plenty of offers from them to take in our Irish setter, but not our family. That was not a nice experience.

John Brown's

Janet Baxter (née Stewart)

A LETTER FROM THE BOSS

Before the war, Old Kilpatrick was a lovely place, and a great place to bring up children. It was all country and Lusset Glen was kept in beautiful condition, although the children had the utmost freedom to play there. You were never checked for anything. In the summer time, we played in the glen from morning till night. Everything came in its season, of course: playing in the glen, the cricket, peever and so on, all the things that children did in those days. Your parents didn't have any fear of anybody interfering with you or anything like that. We went to the glen in the morning and sometimes we weren't back till six o'clock at night.

When the war broke out in 1939 I was twenty one and was working in the drawing office in Denny's in Dumbarton. In a way, I had lost touch with the village by that time because for instance I played badminton in the town and that kind of thing and I was very interested in the trade union and I went to a lot of things concerning it.

My father came in that night at teatime and he said, 'Everybody in the yard (in Scotstoun) is saying this is the night we're going to get it.' It was a beautiful day, sunny and then a moonlit night and we, of course, poo-hooed the idea. My husband was in the navy and I knew he was getting home at the weekend, so I hurried up and did all the housework ready for him coming. I had on my old skirt and just had washed my hair and turned on the wireless when the sirens went at night. So I got my father and the old man who lived next door and we just had to go down to the bottom floor. There was a shop there, run by an old couple, and their house was at the back shop. I put my father and the other old man under a table and the old couple and me went under the bed. This was in Dumbarton Road, the red sandstone building with a white bit in the middle. It was the village shop, that sold everything from groceries to china.

We were nearest to the bomb as could be seen when all the debris was cleared up, but it was the people in the next close who were injured or killed. I don't know how many were killed. I was buried right up to my neck. My father somehow or other seemed to be able to make an opening immediately where they were and he and the old man got out. He shouted to the ARP people, telling them where to come and dig for me. Then they started to dig. I don't know how long they took, because you don't know what time is in that situation. I just said to myself, 'My head's free. I can breathe.'

Actually what had happened was there had been a lull and we had all gone outside. We saw that oil from the oil tanks had run over the canal and it was alight and there were incendiary bombs all over the street. It was just like being in hell to tell you the truth. Then it had started up again and we had gone back into our positions. It had turned cold and the lady had given me the quilt off the bed. I had it wrapped round me up to my neck, which was a good thing because that was the bit that was free when I finally came to.

So, I was eventually dug out and I was put in an ambulance. We thought we were going to the hospital, but we weren't. We were taken to the church hall in Old Kilpatrick. When we got there, the doctor, a young man who was sitting his finals the next day, examined me. My head had got knocked, but he said there was nothing seriously wrong with me. And you felt that was true when there were people lying with broken legs in front of you. So we were just left and I was given, much to my disgust, a pair of sandshoes, black and white, what we called salt and pepper sandshoes. And that's when I burst into tears. I said to them, 'No I don't want them.' My married sister and her husband lived further down the village. So, I said, 'Oh, John'll come and carry me down to the house.'

But, when he appeared, he said, 'I'll do nothing of the kind!' So, on the sandshoes went and I walked to my sister's. Her neighbour made potted hough and toast for us, and there's never a meal will ever taste as sweet as that potted hough and toast! My sister gave me shoes, and then my father discovered he hadn't shoes either, so the man next door gave him shoes although they were a bit big for him – he was a small man.

The next thing, we got word that there was an unexploded bomb behind the building, so we were all to get out. So, from there, the three of us set off and we walked to Drumoyne to John's mother's house. I stayed there till Saturday and then I went down to an aunt in Kirn for a week. By the time I came back, my sister and her husband had managed to get a house in St Kenneth Drive just at Drumoyne, a terraced house where we could all go. It meant we were all together in the one house. The only thing was I had a terrible travel to Dumbarton from there. I got the bus at quarter past seven to Govan Cross, then the subway, then the train to Dumbarton. And the station in Dumbarton is not near Denny's. So it was a long travel every day. It was a few weeks before I went back to work and the boss was not pleased. He said that the chief draughtsman was going to send me a letter and I said – I don't know where I got the strength to say it because in those days you didn't answer back- that, if he did I would take the letter straight to Davie Kirkwood, who was the MP for Clydebank at that time, and was working hard for the people who had been bombed out. I did get support from the girls in the office, my friends, but by that time I had drawn myself together.

Isa McKenzie (née Cameron)

WE ARE NOW AT WAR WITH GERMANY

The things I remember most about the first eighteen months of the war were the black-out and the sandbags that just seemed to have grown overnight round the bases of buildings; and the patterns made by fawn coloured sticky tape in the windows of Council and business premises; and, of course, the big brick baffle walls built at the entrance to every close to reduce the blast from falling bombs. I don't think there was anyone in that town who couldn't tell a tale of walking into one of them.

Soon we all had our National Identity Card (you had to memorise your N.I. number) and our Ration Book. Things started to go short in the shops and people started to join queues sometimes without knowing what they were for, but realising it meant something had arrived at that shop that was considered inessential and was therefore worth waiting for.

One thing in particular from that period that stands out in my mind is standing in a big, long queue outside a church hall to have our gas masks fitted and being shown how to use them. They were repulsive – the feel of the black rubber and the horrid sensation when you had them on. The poor babies! They had to be placed inside what looked like the capsules deep-sea divers use. They must have been terrified.

There was a great upsurge of uniforms in the town, with Home Guards, A.R.P. and, of course, all the young men being called up. My eldest brother had been in the Merchant Navy for a number of years and my folks worried even more about him now.

You lay in bed either waiting for sleep or being wakened from it by the sound of aeroplane engines overhead, arguing with your brother whether it was theirs or ours. We used to say we could tell by the different noise and throb of the engines. There certainly was a difference but whether we allocated it the right country is debatable. Then your heart started to pound when the sirens went off.

By the thirteenth of March 1941, we had had a lot of air raids. As a matter of fact, one week we had them five nights in a row. As we

lived on the top storey of a three storey building, when the sirens went we were allowed to shelter in the hallway of a family on the bottom floor. The air-raid shelters were still in the process of being built in the middle of the streets – no parking problems to be resolved in those days.

It was a beautiful, dry, moonlight night and my brother and I were all ready to go to bed. The sirens blew, so we had to get dressed again, finishing with the Sunday coat which is what we always did. I'll never forget that coat. It was a dusky pink material, with brown fur around the neck and down to the waist. It was fastened by a button at the waist and a toggle-shaped cloth strap at the neck. I always thought, and still do, it was one of the loveliest things I ever had. As I had been playing with a pair of my big sister's court shoes on just before getting ready for bed, I just put them on again. If my mother had been at home, this would not have been allowed, but she had gone to visit a sick friend in another part of the town and had been expected back shortly. The shoes were just a little too big for me, but after all it wouldn't be long until we were home again, would it? So, having picked up the brown leather Gladstone bag which held birth and marriage certificates, insurance policies and any other important documents, and, having collected our gas masks, we headed downstairs.

Before long, the Blitz in all its horror was well underway, and a very brave lady of the A.R.P. had taken up a stance near the entrance to our close. When she heard the whistle of a bomb on its way down, she would shout 'duck!' and the crowd, who must have numbered twenty in the small hallway, would crouch down together, praying it would not have our number on it. When the bang and the blast were over, we would be given the 'OK' to rise again. I have often wondered if that lady survived. I certainly never saw her again.

There were two doors, one leading into the kitchen and the other into the room directly opposite. As they rattled badly every time a bomb fell, a bright spark thought it would be a good idea to tie a rope between each handle. Guess what. The next time a bomb fell the doors blew off their hinges and landed on top of us all.

We remained there for the first five hours wondering if it was ever going to end. Then we were told we had to move out. The building was going up in flames! What we thought was the noise of slates falling from the roof was actually incendiary bombs landing.

Coming out into the street was like taking part in a horror film. There was the noise of planes and fire engines and buildings collapsing and people running, screaming. Fires were everywhere you looked. We made for the half-finished brick air-raid shelters in the middle of the street, but although the walls were finished, the foot-wide concrete roof arches still had wide gaps between them waiting to be filled with cement and, of course, sparks were falling in through these spaces. So, once more we were on the move and someone shouted to head for the billiard room whose back entrance was at the end of our street.

On our way there, we were sure we were being strafed by a plane. No one would believe us but the next day we could see the bullet holes on the side of the building.

Inside the billiard room, we found lots of people with the same idea. The children were put under the tables while wardens and volunteers were bringing in the elderly. I remember an old lady being carried in on her own mattress and placed on the table above us. We were told she was very ill.

The proprietors of a wee shop in our street came round with boxes of biscuits and bottles of lemonade to cheer us up a bit. The helpers would be asked what was going on above – if such and such a close or a particular relative was still safe, but in the children's minds, the most important question was, had the school got it? There were visions of a nice long holiday if the school got a direct hit.

When the all-clear sounded, we emerged into the dawn of a new day, and were stunned to find we could not go home. It had been gutted by fire. So we went further along the street to where our married sister, husband and two children lived in a single end. They were all safe, apart from having no windows and there being mounds of soot over everything.

Just at that moment, our mother appeared safe and sound. She related how she had been on her way home when it all began and had to go into a public shelter and stay there all night.

It was a terrible experience for us children to look at where our house had been. What it must have meant to our parents, having worked hard to build our home and cleaned and polished it for nearly twenty seven years, is hard to imagine. We were all standing there with nothing but the clothes on our backs and not another possession. It was a blessing we still had each other and were not like some families who had lost their nearest and dearest.

David Munn

COMMUNAL RADIO

I was eight years old and lived on the third floor of a four storey tenement in Crown Avenue at the top of Kilbowie Road overlooking the Singer factory. My father was a War Reserve policeman – what would today be known as a Special Constable – and at each and every air raid warning was required to don his uniform and get to the police station in Hall Street for instructions.

The people who lived on the top floor above us were the only people who had a radio (battery operated since there was no electricity supply to the building). We had gas lighting and a gas ring for cooking, though most of our meals were prepared on the coal fire. The aforementioned family used to open their door at one o'clock for the people in our close to squeeze into their lobby to hear the BBC news as to how the war was progressing. If I was present, I would look round in wonderment at these people because they seemed to be understanding what the radio was saying – I could not, because I had never heard the rapid, clipped speech of an English newsreader. When the siren sounded, most of the people from our stairway took refuge, as we had done before, in a kind of windowless cellar just off the common close. We sat on the floor or any object that could be sat on and, for what seemed an eternity, listened to a hail of bombs. These were incendiary bombs, cylindrical things about 18 inches long. Wherever one got stuck in a rone gutter it would immediately burn through slate or tile and set fire to the roof. They burned with a blinding white light for several minutes. There was also the occasional loud crump of a heavier bomb which caused the floor and walls of the cellar to heave.

When the bombers had gone and daybreak was near, everyone went to their houses to see what damage had been done. In my house, the whole frame of the front window had been blown in with such force that it had cut the living room door in half horizontally like a stable door. The flying wreckage had burst its way through the bedroom door along with some bits of brick and plaster. It may well have been the window frame of the house upstairs which killed the three occupants. They had not joined the rest of us in the cellar – or perhaps were just a moment too slow in getting out. I was forbidden to go upstairs. The rest of the day was spent carrying buckets of plaster and broken crockery downstairs and trying to salvage what food we could. I remember my mother scraping plaster off the butter in its dish. My father was, of course, on duty in Clydebank and totally unable to come home except for a quick visit later in the day to see if my mother and I had survived. He had seen the flames coming from the top of the hill but was far too busy shifting stone blocks and dragging people out – dead or half alive. The fires he saw were in fact in Crown Avenue, but a bit further up from where we were.

Our water supply was still intact, but the gas had been turned off somewhere. Mother and I bedded down in the room which still had a window, but we were not left in peace for long. The siren sounded and once again, the inhabitants of the close, minus the top floor family, squeezed into the cellar. This time there were many heavy bombs and the crashing of masonry made it evident that the building was collapsing. Many were the wails and screams and someone was invoking the aid of the Almighty. My own head was exposed and I was aware – and afraid – of two separate fires nearby. I had great pain in my left hip and my left arm was trapped, but fortunately not such as to cut off the blood supply completely.

Mother and I were the first to be rescued by ARP men. We were bundled on to a bus which was crammed with injured people and taken by a devious route – in order to avoid bomb craters – to the Western Infirmary, Glasgow where I had a dislocated hip attended to, as well as my bottom teeth which had been displaced backwards. It was decided to remove a tooth at each side, leaving the four front teeth in their new position. Thus I have rather a peculiar bite, that is, the top teeth overlap the bottom ones. Mother had a broken ankle and very bad bruising, especially about her face.

On release from hospital, walking with sticks and my face bandaged up like the invisible man, we got a bus to the village of Symington, Lanarkshire, where my aunt and grandfather kindly housed us for the next eleven months. Some weeks elapsed before I was fit to go to the village school.

My father was at work for up to sixteen hours a day in Clydebank and

Dalmuir, heaving rubble aside and pulling out people, dead and alive, sometimes from buildings which were in imminent danger of collapsing. He was billeted along with other War Reserve policemen and ARP men who had lost their homes, on camp beds in the Pavilion Theatre at the foot of Kilbowie Road. When finally he managed to visit us he came in police uniform – he had nothing else to wear. We salvaged nothing except the torn and bloodstained clothing we had on.

Father had found out that five more of our neighbours had survived the collapse of the cellar. Two of these were old people, both of whom died some time later, whether as a direct result of their injuries or from shock I know not. Some of my father's team were issued with rifles to shoot cats and dogs. Many of them were injured, were liable to attack, and were feeding from dead bodies. This was just an aside to the grisly work which went on for weeks, of collecting and identifying bodies, when identification was possible. There is a large communal grave in Dalnottar Cemetery containing unidentified remains.

Despite the two nights of bombing, there was little damage to the dockyards or the Singer factory, though the oil tanks burned for a fortnight.

May Fraser

HOMEWARD JOURNEY

It was Thursday 13th March and my fiance Jack and I were enjoying a film show in the Pavilion Cinema at the foot of Kilbowie Road.

It would be well into the evening, perhaps around nine o'clock, when the sirens started wailing. At first we paid little attention for the sirens had been sounding for more than a week every night prior to the air-raid and they had all been false alarms. This time it was very different. We realised bombs were falling and decided to make for my home in Dalmuir West. I knew my mother would be on her own and I wanted to be with her.

Outside the cinema in Kilbowie Road, we found a very brilliant moonlight night. Guns were firing and their tracer bullets were streaking across the sky. We went round by Rosebery Place and made for the main road to Dalmuir West. By this time the concentrated bombing raid was

Singer's showing workers at stopping time

in full swing. Singer's woodyard was blazing, the sparks from the wood blowing in all directions. The streets were littered with broken glass. When we reached the open ground between Clydebank and Dalmuir, we decided to take cover in a shelter opposite the Union Church. A soldier and a sailor had the same idea, but unfortunately the shelter was locked and we took shelter behind the baffle wall. There the four of us had to stay for a long time. Brown's yard was on the left, Singer's behind us and the Royal Ordnance factory at Dalmuir on our right.

As the bombs rained down we instinctively crouched down, the three men determined that I wouldn't be on top of the heap if the wall came down on top of us. There was a gap at the bottom of the wall to let the blast through and I could feel the wind whipping round my legs. We could look out on to the street and we saw a tram car on its way to the west. I often wonder if it ever reached the terminus.

Canaries and budgies were flying about and a number of dogs raced past in panic. Their poor paws would be cut to ribbons. Fireside rugs had been blown out of the houses and were draped over the overhead tram wires. We saw the model lodging house getting a direct hit, and I believe a lot of people lost their lives in there.

By this time we decided to make a dash for my home and after saying goodbye and wishing our soldier and sailor good luck, we started out, using the houses on either side of the main road to dive in and out of closes. On one occasion we landed in somebody's house in their lobby up against a pile of coats. After that experience, we started out again and saw a pall of thick black smoke away to the west and thought the whole place was blazing. Then we realised it was the oil tanks at Old Kilpatrick that had been hit.

There was still a bit to go before we got to Castle Square and at one point we dashed into the close next to the post office and a pile of masonry fell at our heels. We couldn't get back out to the street but went round the back and out the next close. A naval ship in the river had been firing her big guns and an added hazard was the red hot lumps of shrapnel thumping into buildings, lamp posts and anything in their path.

At last we made it to the corner and turned into Castle Square and home. At that point, we saw a landmine floating down attached to a parachute. It seemed to be heading in the direction of Jellicoe Street.

At home, we found all the neighbours in our building were in our house including a number of children. We had a bottom flat with a long narrow lobby from the front door to the bathroom. It was thought to be the safest part of the building. We had no shelter to go to, and that had been the arrangement. Nobody had been injured and even the children remained remarkably quiet. I think exhaustion had taken over. My mother was very relieved to see us safely home, and Jack and I were glad to sit down on the floor to spend the rest of a very long night.

The bombs came down in clusters of seven and you automatically counted the explosions, some of them very close indeed. At around six o'clock the all clear sounded. But prior to that Jack said to me, 'One of the bombs hasn't gone off and I think it's very near.' We were getting up off the floor when the bomb did go off. The house actually lifted then settled. I remember the lino ripping right across the floor. Then blessed quiet and a stillness.

Our neighbours went home and Jack went to Parkhall to see how his family had fared. We soon realised that everybody in our building was leaving to stay with friends and we would be the only two left. Everybody said the Germans would be back to finish what they had started.

I went out to see what damage had been done and discovered the last bomb had brought down the building in Castle Street and the dead bodies were laid out on the pavement covered in sheets. Mrs Johnstone was one of them, the President of the Parish Church Women's Guild. The shelter between our house and the main road was flattened and everybody in it died. Young Betty Quig, aged 17 and an only child, went to the shelter for safety while her parents remained in their top storey flat. The dead bodies were laid out in our backcourt.

Jellicoe Street took an awful pounding and I remember an elderly gentleman standing gazing at the remains of the street. His entire family had been holding a family party on the thirteenth and were all killed. The old man was their grandfather, the family the Rocks.

My mother and I decided to get to Ayr to our relatives, and before we left, I went to Parkhall to see how Jack's family had fared. They had no damage and decided to stay put. They had an Anderson shelter in the garden. I later learned that Jack spent the second night kicking incendiary bombs off the roof, but to no avail. The house went up in flames for all his efforts to save it.

My mother and I filled a case and made for Ayr, leaving all our possessions open to the elements. Anything on wheels was taking people – the lorry drivers were especially helpful.

That night, the 14th, I lay in my aunt's bedroom and listened to the drone of the planes making for my home town and I prayed for the lives of all who had to endure another night of Hell.

The next day I phoned my office in Glasgow to let them know I had survived, and needed some time to see what was to happen at home. When I got to Dalmuir, I found 2 Castle Square in a very dangerous condition and was advised that our belongings would be stored in the La Scala Cinema along with countless others until required again.

Many of the original people never came back again and to my mind, Clydebank and Dalmuir were never the same.

Denis Kearns

CHAPPIE TOOK THE MICKEY

It was a mild spring evening in 1939 when our family made its way to St James' Church Hall. The church, which stood a few yards east of the Empire Picture House on Glasgow Road, was one of a number of designated gas mask distribution centres which had been set up throughout Clydebank and neighbouring villages.

Having reached my fourth birthday, I failed to qualify for a 'Mickey Mouse' gas mask. I was not the least bit pleased! However, my displeasure turned to downright jealousy on seeing that my diminutive three-year-old pal, Chappie French, had hit the jackpot!

As both families made their way back to their homes in Whitecrook that evening I continued to voice my disappointment. As we passed Mrs McGregor's house at No. 3 East Barns Street she bade us a cheery 'Good evening' and added, 'What's wrong with Denis?'

Before anyone could answer I bellowed, 'Chappie French got a Mickey Mouse gas mask and I didnae! It looks nothing like Mickey Mouse – it's rubbish!'

As for poor wee Chappie, christened Hugh Peter Anthony, he was oblivious to my jealous outburst. It was after all, well past his bedtime and he was by that time fast asleep in his pushchair.

This was only one of a whole catalogue of humorous incidents and anecdotes my mother used to recall many years after that dramatic build-up to World War II, the war years themselves and their aftermath. As well as having a quite remarkable sense of humour, she was blessed with a sharp and retentive memory into her old age.

THE FIRST EVACUATION

Despite the clouds of the gathering storm, the summer of 1939 saw thousands of families throughout the country make their way to their favourite coastal holiday resorts. For many Glasgow and West of Scotland folk that invariably meant heading 'doon the watter' to the Clyde Coast

Saltcoats 1939: Denis Kearns second from right with sisters Margaret and Catherine, and cousin Ian Fraser

holiday towns of their choice.

For our family, and no doubt for many others, that one holiday was to hold a special place in our memories. As the youngest of my parents' eight children, that July holiday in Saltcoats was the first that I could recall with any degree of detail. It was also, sad to say, the last holiday we would share together as a family. Who would have guessed then that by the end of that beautiful summer many of those same families would be caught up in the trauma of a nation-wide evacuation which would see an estimated 3.5 million children on the move?

Even as a four-year-old I have vivid memories of that first day of The Evacuation. For us children, it was just one big exciting adventure. We learn from Our Holy Redeemer's school log (head master's diary) of Friday 1st September 1939 that 893 children and 151 mothers left that morning – destination Helensburgh. However, as Mr Francis McGuire did not specify the number of accompanied pre-school children included in that figure, it was generally thought that somewhere in the region of 40 per cent of the school roll was evacuated that day.

In order to assist the educational needs of such a large influx of evacuees into the Helensburgh area something like 30 per cent of the school's fairly large teaching staff had been transferred to St Joseph's R.C. Primary and Hermitage Academy just prior to the evacuation. These teachers accompanied the mothers and children as far as Helensburgh Central railway station that morning. I certainly felt very grown up with my gas mask over my shoulder, and my pinned-on name tag, marching to and from railway stations with all those big boys and girls.

As the three eldest members of our family had left school it was therefore along with her five youngest children that our mother alighted from the LMS 'Evacuee Special' around 11.00 a.m. that day. After forming a large column we were split into two groups. Our group went to Clyde Street School, the other Victoria Halls. Both these locations were designated 'Evacuee Reception Centres.'

Twice a Billeting Officer offered my mother accommodation that would have necessitated splitting up the family. Twice she declined the offer.

Having spent the best part of two hours in John Street school we were taken up to the Victoria Halls in Sinclair Street. By mid afternoon, we were only one of three family groups still to be billeted. Conscious of the fact that her youngest charge was getting more and more restless by the minute, my mother decided that come 4.00 p.m. we would call it a day and return to Clydebank.

The Hill House: Helensburgh

It was then that Miss Agnes Blackie, who was acting on behalf of her father, offered us accommodation. However, when she saw our Catherine she said, 'I am very sorry Mrs Kearns, but my father doesn't want a mixed family.'

On hearing these words, Catherine burst into tears. Miss Agnes, thoroughly embarrassed at the situation that had developed, apologised and told my mother that she would clear the situation with her father, and come back in ten minutes. 'I am sure it will be alright,' she added.

THE HILL HOUSE: A HOME FROM HOME

When we arrived at The Hill House in the Blackie family car that afternoon, Miss Agnes introduced us to her parents who quickly put us at our ease. She then showed us to the kitchen where the cook had already prepared afternoon tea.

The Hill House, when my family knew it, was set against a beautiful backdrop of mature woodland of Scots pine and firs interspersed with some native species of broad leaves. The wood abounded in wildlife, for what it lacked in depth it made up for in density and peripheral ground cover. For bird lovers, the constant cooing of a prolific colony of wood-pigeons gave The Hill House and neighbouring homes a rather special atmosphere. Alas, the hurricane which devastated the West of Scotland one night in 1968 destroyed all but a handful of those beautiful trees.

It was shortly after the turn of the century that Walter Blackie, the book publisher, commissioned the now celebrated Scottish architect, Charles Rennie Mackintosh, to design and build a house for him in the upper reaches of Helensburgh. That house at number 8 Upper Colquhoun Street he aptly named 'The Hill House.' Today it is under the auspices of the National Trust for Scotland.

Later that day Mrs Blackie informed my mother that she and Mr Blackie had decided to make additional accommodation available and extended an invitation to my father and the rest of our family to join us at weekends. This they did.

The following afternoon, Saturday 2nd September they arrived. Mary, the eldest had turned nineteen; Pat, slightly younger, had left school and was about to start reading English and Philosophy at Glasgow University. The third member of the trio, Margaret, like Mary was working in

Clydebank. She had just turned sixteen.

As we entered the now redundant servants' and tradesmen's entrance on Kennedy Drive my mother introduced my father to Mr Will Howe whom we had met on our way down to the railway station. Mr Howe, addressed by the Blackies as 'Howe', was Mr Blackie's resident gardener. He was an extremely experienced and hard-working man with young teenage twin daughters, Carrie and Grace and son William. Tragically, Mrs Howe died very suddenly just prior to her young family moving to the Hill House in the early thirties.

Like my father, Will Howe had survived the horrors and hardships of that 'war to end wars,' Will in the Seaforth Highlanders, my father in the Black Watch. From that first meeting, those two not-so-old soldiers became firm friends.

The following day our family gathered round a wireless set in the schoolroom which was situated in the upper east wing of the house. Although I was much too young to understand what all the fuss was about, I could nevertheless sense the seriousness of the occasion which called for such utter silence. They were, of course, listening to Neville Chamberlain's historic address to the nation.

I have often wondered what must have been going through the anxious minds of our parents that day. My father had tried so hard to put the horrors of that war behind him. He and my mother had put their romance on hold for the duration of that dreadful experience while she, in turn, had served in the Women's Land Army during its final two years.

Little could they have foreseen that day that before the end of this Second World War, three of their teenage children would also be in uniform. Pat joined the Local Defence Volunteers (LDV), the forerunner of the Home Guard, prior to joining the Royal Air Force in June 1941. Margaret joined the army (ATS) the following year, while Hugh followed Pat into the Air Force as we entered the final year of the war. While he completed his training as an air gunner, Hugh was spared the danger of operational flying as Germany surrendered some four weeks later. Even Mary did her stint in uniform during the last two years of the war, although for Mary, it was in the uniform of an auxiliary nurse at Mearnskirk Military Hospital.

So there we were, two Scottish families at war. Two families, a generation apart, from opposite ends of the social scale under one roof.

Two families, one Catholic and working class, the other Protestant and upper-middle class, both united in their determination to resist the biggest evil this world has ever encountered – Hitler and the barbaric Fascist regime of Nazi Germany.

It was a beautiful late autumn evening in 1939 when my parents took their youngest child for a short walk around the 'Skater's Pond' known locally as the Frog Pond. During those frequent strolls, they would always call into 'The Walker's Rest', a little public park adjacent to what was then the town's water filtration and purification works at the top of Sinclair Street. Often as not, my big brothers Jim and Tom could be found in the thick of things playing football or rounders. The latter, based roughly on baseball rules, was very popular among the young evacuees in Upper Helensburgh.

Still there to this day, that little park invariably echoed to the laughter and excited screams of evacuated children at play. The 'Rest' which remained standing until just a few years ago, was in the form of a small open-fronted wooden hut with a continuous bench running along its three sides.

During nice weather and pleasant evenings, mothers would escape with their children and knitting from the sometimes quite restrictive and austere atmosphere of their wartime billets and head for The Walker's Rest. It was while returning from the latter that particular evening that Ruth Blackie introduced us to her husband, Major Hederwick. He was apparently spending his embarkation leave at The Hill House prior to joining his unit in France.

As we said farewell and walked toward the house I asked my father, 'Why is Major Hederwick wearing a belt across his chest?'

'That's his Sam Brown,' replied my father.

'Well, if that's Sam Brown's belt, why is Major Hederwick wearing it?' says I.

My mother, who had a very infectious and high-pitched laugh, which on occasion could tend towards a bit of a scream, was so embarrassed that she felt obligated to explain her sudden outburst to Mrs Hederwick and her husband. No doubt to her considerable relief, they too thought it a huge joke.

When we returned to The Hill House after the Clydebank Blitz we were very saddened to hear Major Hederwick had been killed in France. For the Blackie family and Mrs Hederwick that war during the early summer of 1940 had been anything but 'phoney.'

It was at the beginning of that year that we bade a fond farewell to the Blackie family and returned to the somewhat less than spacious confines of our wee three bedroom council house in the east end of Clydebank. Like Dorothy in that recently-viewed picture 'The Wizard of Oz' we all agreed that 'there's no place like home.'

I think it was true to say that such was the extreme inconvenience and disruption to family life caused by that first evacuation that few, if any, of that large contingent of evacuees remained in Helensburgh after the spring of 1940.

TIG'S THE NAME OF THE GAME

By that late summer the so-called 'phoney war' in Europe was well and truly over. The battle for Britain's survival had begun as mothers left their bemused five year-olds in the caring charge of infant teacher, Mrs O'Donnell.

I didn't like the experience one wee bit and resolved to make a dash for it at the earliest opportunity. That moment came during my very first playtime when I discovered that the small wrought iron gate between the infant playground and Our Holy Redeemer's Church was unlocked.

However, my great escape to Whitecrook was short-lived as my big brother, Pat, marched his protesting and tearful wee brother back down the road to that horrible school again.

A few days later I came to the conclusion that school wasn't such a bad place after all. I particularly liked the frenetic hurly-burly of playtime and, above all else, the game of TIG. The excitement of the chase from that dreaded infant who was deemed to be 'HET' or 'hit' was great fun! Sanctuary lay beyond the entrance to that extremely wet and smelly open-air toilet which the janitor, Mr Durning, would dutifully hose out each afternoon.

'Hee, Hee, Hee, ye cannae tig me!' was the defiant chant which would resound from that appalling school toilet as those incredibly fleet of foot children would cross its threshold.

Seven months later, the start of my primary school education was abruptly suspended. Little did I know just how often that particular place of refuge would come back to haunt me.

I dedicate this poem to the memory of those many innocent children and adults who were killed during the Clydebank Blitz, those many others who died later as a result of their injuries, and those whose lives were adversely affected by trauma and bereavement.

RECURRING NIGHTMARE

No awesome wailing from sirens
Disturbs my cosy sleep
No laboured drones from Heinkels
Heavy laden with bombs
No smell from burning candle
No night-long vigils of prayer
No warmth radiates from tiny stove
Nor dampness from earthen floor
No crashing of nearby gables
Shock-waves or deafening bangs
No reassuring shouts of neighbours
Defiant banter during lulls
No mugs of hot sweet tea
Nor cuddles through the night
No pungent odour of cordite
Hangs heavy in still morning air
Only a ghostly silence
Heralds that dreaded apparition's return
I run towards my place of refuge
Leaden feet and muted screams
That large aeroplane silently follows
With bomb doors open wide
Stops motionless above my head
Rooted to the spot

No bombs ever fall
No 'All-clear' ever sounds
I awake.

RETURN TO THE HILL HOUSE

On returning to The Hill House, we were surprised to see that Mr Blackie had had a 'luxury' air-raid shelter built in our absence. I certainly couldn't think of a more apt word to describe it. Having been designed and constructed to his own specifications, it was situated a couple of feet from the rear of the house and almost flush with the west gable end. Built with four courses of brick with a baffle wall protecting its heavy steel door, its reinforced concrete roof was sandbagged as was the outside of the baffle wall. Inside it had a W.C. and wash-hand-basin, an electric cooker, a wood-burning stove and electric lighting. Finished with a course of roughcast and painted to match the house I've no doubt that even Rennie Mackintosh would have been tempted to give it his seal of approval.

I think it was at the beginning of April 1941 that we first took to the shelter. Along with the servants and Mr Howe's family, were Mr & Mrs Blackie, Miss Agnes and Mrs Hederwick. My father, Mr Howe and a gardener from further down Upper Colquhoun Street called Mr John George had formed a local fire watching team. They were out on their rounds.

A month later came the Greenock and Port Glasgow Blitz. Unlike the Clydebank Blitz in mid March, dawn broke much earlier at the beginning of May. As the all-clear sounded after the first night's raid we all returned to our rooms. From the highest vantage point in Helensburgh, The Hill House's school room, we looked down on an awesome sight. The whole of Greenock and Port Glasgow seemed to be alight. What made the sight of all those fires all the more awesome was that they were reflected as a mirror image on the Clyde which was as calm as a mill pond. Indeed, at six years of age, I took some convincing that the water was not, in fact, on fire.

A few weeks after that blitz, Pat handed in his Home Guard uniform and rifle and joined the Royal Air Force. He returned to The Hill House for short leaves after his 'square bashing' and basic training. In the early spring of 1942, after completing his flying training in South Africa, he returned once more to Helensburgh – that time on embarkation leave.

It was a beautiful spring Sunday afternoon when Pat decided to take his four young brothers down to The Augusta Lodge Café for whatever they fancied. Sitting looking out of the café window we could see that a large presence of naval personnel was ashore.

Liberty boats were busily coming and going from the pier, obviously from the huge convoy of merchant and naval ships which had gathered at the Tail of the Bank. Motor torpedo boats and corvettes, making their presence felt, were weaving in and out of the convoy while Catalina and Sunderland flying boats on short surveillance circuits kept taking off on full throttle and splashing down like huge inanimate swans. It was a fascinating sight.

Little did we know as we said our farewells to our big brother Pat later that day that it would be almost three and a half years before we would see him again. Days later he joined No. 99 Bomber Squadron in North Africa, a squadron he would remain with until the end of the war with Japan.

FAREWELL TO THE HILL HOUSE

At the beginning of 1943 we bade a fond farewell to the Blackie family, their servants, the beautiful and friendly atmosphere of The Hill House and Helensburgh itself and returned to our little council house in the bomb-battered east end of Clydebank. Our return was shortly followed by my homesick sister Catherine who had worked as a maid for Mrs Blackie for two years.

Though we all felt a pang of sadness leaving such a pleasant environment, home is where the heart is, and that Dirty Old Town, bomb-battered or not, was where we wanted to be.

But oh, how it had changed! Of the first 44 houses in our street, East Barns Street, only 8 remained standing, and of those, three lay derelict until the summer of 1944.

On to 'D Day' and that summer of 1944 and the growing belief that it would only be a matter of time before we'd be hanging out, not our washing on the Siegfried Line, but victory flags in our streets. As one prisoner of war after another started to come back to the town, so too did the anticipation of Germany's inevitable surrender grow. Huge bonfires were erected early in preparation for Victory in Europe Day, a day and night none of us will ever forget.

However, despite the nation-wide euphoria which sparked off all those wonderful street parties, many families were still very much aware that the war in the Far East against that most war-like of nations, Japan, was still very much ongoing.

Let us hope and pray that we will never forget all those who fought in that epic battle for democracy, or the many brave souls who laid down their lives in order that we might live in peace – a peace which we must never take for granted.

Charles Clunas

ME AND THE CLYDEBANK BLITZ

In March 1941, when German bombers destroyed my home town of Clydebank, I was roughly fifteen, living in Johnstone, west of Paisley and completely cocooned in that spiritual myopia typical, I would like to think, of boys of that age. I was completely bound up in my chums, cycling round Renfrewshire, girls of my own age, the youth club I had a share in keeping going, homework, getting on at school and sharing the care of my uncle's racing pigeons. It is not really a very long list, but had enough in it to soak up virtually all of my attention as to the world around me. I have started my story in this way in an attempt to explain what was the very low level of my emotional involvement in Clydebank's greatest disaster, which damaged all but 26 of its homes, utterly destroyed most of the rest, killed a thousand of its people and badly injured another thousand, displaced virtually all the rest, and, in short, produced an irreversible upheaval in the town's life and geography. I swanned through this as through a film set, oblivious in myself to the fact that our family had been literally inches away from losing my father (and therefore our livelihood) and all our worldly possessions. It was a real enough experience for others.

By that March our family (that is, my mother, sister and I, and intermittently my father) had been living for eighteen months in Johnstone, the home town of both my parents. My father had been blacklisted in the 20s from working at his trade as tool-fitter there, and he had got himself into the Singer's Sewing Machine factory in Clydebank by keeping mum about his union membership. When the war broke out they had been living at 398 Dumbarton Road, Clydebank for ten years, but as Johnstone exiles. By September 1939, a decision had been made to evacuate the three of us back to Johnstone while my father stayed at home, kept on at Singer's and commuted on the weekends he was not called on to work. We were encamped rather than installed in the 'big room' of my Uncle Will's two room and kitchen tenement house at 4 Gleniffer Terrace, Johnstone, sharing it with my widower uncle and my cousin Annie. Annie was in her early twenties and "kept the house" until my mother arrived and relieved her of some of the duties so that she could do her War Work and earn money.

The Phoney War had passed with no bombing at all in our part of the world and there had grown up a quiet disbelief that we would ever be included in the global conflict at all. However, the Ministry of Information and what news was allowed to percolate through to the public kept us aware that bombing, sirens going off, and general disturbance in the middle of the night was still on the cards. Left to myself I don't know if I would have noticed – I had my homework to do for one thing and Anna Hughes was giving me a favourable smile or two for another – but my mother organised some kind of order. When we went to bed we had to lay out on the floor the clothes we had taken off, ready to be jumped into at a moment's notice. Our close was immediately round the corner from the ground floor room and kitchen in Williamson Place occupied by my married cousin Nan and her husband. The kitchen was protected on the south by Gleniffer Terrace and on the north by a stone staircase to the second storey over the next-door pend. The theory then was that Nan's kitchen was a lot safer than ours, stuck as it was up in the air. I suppose if the building had ever collapsed we would have been smothered without hope of rescue but as Johnstone was never bombed this was never tested.

We had had some scares, false alarms or otherwise over a period of some months beforehand and had been terrified during such events by some terrific explosions which shook the earth Nan's house was built on. This was so nearly what we thought bombs would be like that we were amazed to find the next mornings that there was no devastation being reported, either officially or on the grapevine. The latter was not to be trusted too much but was better than the radio or newspaper reports, partly because it was an open secret that bad news was always played down and partly because we had a feeling that Johnstone was such a minor player on the world stage that we were hardly worth mentioning. However, the grape-vine did eventually report that the shaking was caused by a 'big gun' at Elderslie three or four miles down the road and we felt we were being protected rather than exposed. I have no way of knowing what the German aircraft were doing over the West of Scotland during those months to get us out of our beds at two in the morning – reconnaissance for the blitz in March, perhaps, but it did enable us to get a system going at a touch, dressing smartly and whispering our way down to Nan's kitchen. This whispering was pretty much a psychological thing as if we didn't want to waken those around us, who presumably were oblivious to the sirens' wailing going on round about and were sleeping soundly through all the droning of aeroplanes and banging of 'big guns.' Of course, there was also the feeling among us that we were stuck in a pretty impressive and dramatic situation and it deserved the condition of awe we were acting up to. At that time, I consistently carried one book or another about with me, ready to open it and improve the shining hour during the bus/ train/ railway journey or on the visit to the dentist. However I didn't take a book with me during air-raid situations. I suppose the thought was that the all-clear was going to go soon and by and large it did, but also that the situation was too significant to be mixed up with a Jeeves story or the like.

On Thursday 13th March 1941 the warning wail of the sirens had us up again shortly after my bed-time and I dutifully clambered into the clothes by my bed and joined in the tip-toeing down to Nan's. The sky was showing a 'bomber's moon' – a full or nearly full moon with a clear sky somewhat obscured by lumps of cloud, so that a bomber pilot looking down would see his target laid out below him once he passed through the cloud, and likewise the anti-aircraft gunners would catch sight of the plane then. We sat around the kitchen table and made idle conversation as usual, expecting to go back up to bed in three-quarters of an hour or so. There were drones and bangs from outside as usual until it dawned on us that not only was it going on longer than usual, it was becoming louder rather than fading away. The Elderslie gun was shaking the ground beneath us as usual, or rather more than usual and even down here in the kitchen it was becoming clear to us that this was not the usual brief interruption to a good night's sleep. Nancy and I were not allowed to go out of doors of course, but my uncle was under no such ban and no doubt felt he would look a bit of a jessie if he stayed cooped up with the women and children all the time. Anyway he had the safety of his pigeon loft to look after. He hardly ever brought any bits of news back with him, mainly because there never was any real news, Johnstone being pretty much ignored as usual. These inhibitions as to bobbing in and out and reporting back to us did not bear on my cousin Nan, our nominal hostess. Her husband, Willie Watt, no doubt considering his sleep in preparation for the morrow's bus driving as having priority, did not get out of his bed on these occasions, and of course he was as safe or unsafe there as we were in the kitchen. Nan was therefore quite free to join the little knot of neighbours inspecting the sky and the horizon and to dash in with the latest as to what 'they' said. 'They say they've dropped bombs up the Braes' or 'They say they're heading home now.'

That night in March, Nan's reports started in much the same way as usual and were received with the same scepticism as usual. However, they went on and on and, what was worse, became more specific and more dreadful. 'They say the Clyde's on fire.' 'They say Glasgow is bombed flat.' As the night wore on Nancy and I became more and more bored. I, in my cocoon (see above), was merely fed up, but the nine-year old Nancy had added to this a degree of fear at the bangs which had gone on shaking the floor. We were sent under the kitchen table in a gesture at coping with the possibility of the bombing spreading and, in a bizarre passage within that time envelope, I started teaching Nancy Latin, and she dutifully joined me in declining mensa, mensa, mensam, mensae etc. (table), which I clearly remember, and other parroting nonsenses which I do not.

The all-clear did not go until about six o'clock I seem to remember and we stumbled out into the dawn not knowing what had happened overnight, but knowing very well that it had been something very significant. Nancy and I did not go to school in the morning – there was a rule about schooling after air-raid warnings (all we had had up till then) whereby we were excused punctuality pro rata to the interruption of our night's sleep.

I am sorry that the rest of my memories over this day and the next two are too vague to set down. My father walked through the smoking rubble that had been Dumbarton or Glasgow Road and crossed the Clyde by the Yoker ferry, which was still able to run and on to Johnstone, walking, tramming and bussing it where he could. I learned that, when he arrived at Gleniffer Terrace, completely shattered, he was immediately offered a glass of whisky to relax him. One hundred per cent teetotaller though he was to my certain knowledge then and afterwards, he drank it down. Remember, he had had no way of knowing but that the bombs had flattened

Johnstone too and that he was the only one to survive. My mother must have been in agony till he arrived, for until he did, there was no knowledge of his survival. Remember, the news of what happened overnight was completely brushed out of radio broadcasts or newspaper reports, which told us nothing more than that, 'there was bombing activity over the West of Scotland last night and *n* German planes were shot down.' There was

Radnor Street, walking towards Kilbowie Road

quite a bit of hostility about this among ordinary people, as somehow proving how unimportant we were to 'them', the Establishment. But I doubt whether we would have been any happier about having true reports of bombing devastation all over industrial Britain coming at us every morning for months on end.

Looking back as a more than middle-aged grandfather and knowing what I know now, I am aghast at my attitude as I remember it. Understanding the horror was beyond me, apparently. It never occurred to me that it was a miracle my father survived to tell the tale – he was such a strong character he was bound to survive, wasn't he? I did not think there was anything at all remarkable about our close (and the next one along) surviving the explosives and incendiaries. In my utterly unthinking cocoon I must have been very easy to deal with, not particularly unsettled in my ways and keeping out from under everyone's feet. The other side of the coin was that I could not appreciate the agony gone through by my mother until my father actually turned up at our house, quite traumatised, nor could I recognise that trauma when he finally appeared. His own family, my grandparents, uncles and aunts at the other end of the town must have had their own terrors. My father's brother Charlie had been the victim of cruel fate on the Somme in 1917 and, until they got word of Alex's safety, there was the chance that the same sort of thing had happened to him 25 years later. And, of course, as far as ordinary working folk were concerned, telephones were well in the future; I don't know how word was sent to his own family at the other end of our small town. Both my mother's and my father's families were not given to shows of emotion and, as far as I can remember, I was encouraged in my lack of deep feeling by the culture round me.

The German bombers came over again the next night but the whole thing was merged into one blur in my mind. Another long night in Nan's kitchen I suppose, another bomber's moon, more rumour-gathering by Nan but thankfully another safe night for Johnstone; perhaps that Latin-beneath-the-table story belongs to the second night. But at least we were all together and safe. And oddly enough, despite the racket, the dropping of thousands of tons of high explosive and incendiary bombs, our close in Clydebank stood through it all. Not quite untouched; as punctilious as ever, my father after his awful night of firefighting, had gone round our wee flat, which had all the windows blown in of course, and closed all the doors to shut out the chaos, no doubt. And on the second night they were all blown in. I cannot remember what happened to my schooling, although I guess every effort was made to have our lives, Nancy's and mine, go on as normally as possible.

Of course, over with us, there was no way of knowing if our house had survived that second night, so when there was no third or fourth night and it seemed safe enough during the daylight hours anyway, it was arranged that my father, my mother and I would go over to see what was what. There was no question but that public transport along the north side of the Clyde did not exist any longer, nor the roads either for that matter, and it was reckoned it would be too much for the nine-year-old Nancy. So off we went, optimistically outwardly anyway, carrying such empty suitcases as we could muster. I remember walking down Glasgow/Dumbarton Road from the ferry at Yoker as if through a Hollywood set, taking it all in visually and indeed intellectually, concentrating on the damage so visible around me, but not taking on board the horror of the human devastation. In the few days since the bombing, any dead bodies had been removed and there had been so much evacuation of survivors out of the area that the only people we saw were the relatively few returners like ourselves and the firemen and others attending to the few spots of smouldering rubble and pulling down some of the towering cliffs of tenement façades which were in danger of collapsing on top of us. My memories are not all clear cut, but I have the impression of it all being much more orderly and tidy, and much less chaotic than I had expected.

The close was there! The flat was there, albeit with the lovely solid doors smashed in. The 'big room' which faced the river over a big wide stretch of plots looked over the same vista as usual, for the naval guns defending the shipyards had done their work well and the riverside industry was hardly damaged. But Dumbarton Road to our west was levelled. When I looked out of the kitchen window up to the hills, the whole vista was terribly changed. Singer's woodyard all along the canal was gone; the Holy City where I had gone to primary school was no more than heaps upon heaps of rubble. The side streets along Dumbarton Road to the west were razed as well. The effect on me was of complete disorientation.

To get back to our house, our idea was to salvage what we needed or valued or whatever. There was no talk of looting, now that I think of it, but then the place was pretty much deserted. Later there was talk of the workmen who were employed to replace the windows and so on, 'taking things' and I seem to remember that we lost some real trivia. I was treated in a very civilised way, I think now, and was told I could take away such of my own possessions as I could carry about my person. The next bit strikes me as odd, or at least smile-able. I had collected a lot of novels in small formats (Collins World Classics and the like) in Ballantyne's annual remainder sales in Paisley. I had also become a Dickens fanatic – this has continued throughout my life but never more so than then – and had a collection of sixpenny editions bought regularly from Woolworth's. As a result, I had acquired a drawer, quite deep but not much more than fifteen inches wide, in the old-fashioned dresser in my Clydebank bedroom, to hold my little library which filled it with about a cubic inch to spare. When I was awarded my concession, I proceeded to shift this collection of trashy editions encasing my spiritual values, into the pockets of my raincoat and jacket. This is a very clear memory – manoeuvring little brown-and-orange bound books into the non-expandable pockets with an intense feeling of hanging on to my values while threatened by the barbarians, and struggling back to Johnstone clad in garments which gave me a distinctly pear shape. And all these years later I keep one or two of these same books on my shelves as part of my secret life.

And so the Blitz was over and we were effectively Johnstonians. I think my father and mother had always had ambitions to move back to their home town; after all when the War started they had been away from it for only ten years, and this looked like a good time to do something to change the situation. As I was as cocooned as ever I was on the outer periphery of the affair, but I know they had sought an interview with either the Provost or the Housing Convener, anyway the Big Man in Johnstone Council housing. I thought this was a big deal, but of course both my parents were well-known left wingers and the Johnstone Town Council, like virtually all those in the West of Scotland, was Labour controlled, so the man they went to see had been known to them for twenty years or more. When they came back, my father's face was like thunder and my mother was a lot less cheery in front of us than her usual self. It had apparently been put to them that if they were not prepared to produce some 'key money' (a contemporary euphemism for a bribe) there was nothing doing. I remember the quotation still: 'Lots of folk would like a council house, you know. Some would give fifty, aye a hundred pounds, for a council house.' Whoever he was he had tried it on with the wrong man; my father had an utter disgust for corruption of any kind, no matter how trivial.

So I didn't grow up a Johnstonian, for we all went home to Clydebank in the summer of 1943. Still, I remember my four-year teenage stay there with fondness and affection.

Ironically, during these years, my father was the least Johnstonian of all. He had to earn his living, of course, and, in the early forties, Singer's was occupied in making armaments (Bren guns, mostly, I think) and was going at it full blast. It may look good in the history books, this matter of getting behind the war effort, but in our family it meant we didn't see much of our father; he worked from 8 a.m. to 8 p.m. on Mondays, Wednesdays and Thursdays, from 8 a.m. to 1 p.m. on those Saturdays when he didn't go till 5.30 and 8 a.m. till 5.30 p.m. every second Sunday. He could visit us in Johnstone only occasionally. Indeed we might have seen more of him in the aggregate if he had been in the RAF and stationed at Parkhead, or even Doncaster, as my father-in-law to be was.

That Golden Age of my childhood was collapsing in ways other than the typical teenage ones. It hadn't been a Golden Age in terms of money (my father had been unemployed some of the time) or psychologically (I enjoyed very little of my year and a half at Clydebank High School) but it was so, all the same, in an even deeper sense. The family was a tight unit – we four ate together, slept in the same wee house, listened to the same radio programmes and so on and so on. I knew where I lived and the culture round me and I knew who were in my circle of chums and who were not. Now my father's occasional bobbing in and out of my life was the beginning of the end, or so it seemed.

After the Blitz there was a time when we did not know but that it would happen again. Although my mother still went back to 398 Dumbarton Road, Dalmuir, our Clydebank home, we youngsters never did, until the war was on the turn and it was considered we could sleep safely through every night. In 1943, then, as I mentioned, once I had got my Highers at Camphill School in Paisley and was going to start at the University of Glasgow, we moved back, lock, stock and barrel and I entered my Grey Period. The history books would have any greyness down to rationing, the blackout and so on, but I never thought they were that bad. I had the appetite of a seventeen-year-old schoolboy and always had enough to eat; I could find my way about in the blackout and, although a lot of things in our culture – education, cinema, libraries, etcetera, etcetera, were marking time, we youngsters did not know this; and the Minister of Information was doing such an effective job that my thinking on the progress of the war was utterly positive. No, the greyness was about the people I moved among, or rather no longer did, from 1943 onwards. The Blitz had killed a lot of the people I knew; such chums as survived were scattered to the four winds or, as time went on, were called to the colours (I myself was on a B.Sc. course and, as such was in a 'reserved occupation').

In short, most of the touchstones of my Clydebank life had crumbled into dust. The McGregor family, who had been the backbone of the Socialist Sunday School and who had lived opposite Yarrow's shipyard at Yoker were wiped out on the first night. Jim Anderson, who spent that Tuesday night as an Air Raid Precautions bicycle messenger got 'home' on the Wednesday morning to find the house, his parents and his five sisters wiped off the face of the earth. My close chum, Jim Kerr, was off to the RAF to be a Flight Engineer and after his post-training leave I never saw him again. My parents' friends, the Geddeses, were living a nomadic life in church halls or the like down about Balloch. The lines of tenements round us had disappeared. The kent faces in the streets were there no longer, and I had to start from scratch making new friendships without the network that I had in 1938; I had not even been to school with the young people I met up with. 'Things fall apart' said the poet and that is what it was like. And viewed from today, the loss I didn't know I had was the result of clothes rationing; where youngsters nowadays can immerse themselves in fashion if their interests so take them, we were stuck this year with what we had bought last, and left dreaming of a jacket we might get next year or even the next again.

This has been a very personal story of course and pretty low key at that. Hardly any tears, screams or hearts engraved with horror as far as I was concerned. I have tried to explain why I remain relatively untouched by the events, but deep deep down, even my minimal dramas must reveal the Clydebank Blitz for the stunning event it was.

Kathleen McConnell

2 NAPIER STREET

I was twelve years old at the time of the Blitz. I lived with my parents, two older brothers and two older sisters in 2 Napier Street. I attended St Margaret's school in Paisley as an 'out-county' pupil, due to the earlier evacuation of Our Holy Redeemer's School.

Thursday the thirteenth of March dawned like any other day. Thirteen an unlucky number? It was for me! I was late for school that morning and had to pay the penalty by staying in at four o'clock to make up the time lost. It didn't bother me too much – there was a good film on at the La Scala and I was going there with my friend Chrissie. Little did I know what was in store for us.

The sirens sounded about nine o'clock. We were at home now except brother Joe who worked in the Bank Cinema in the evenings while he studied to be a Civil Engineer. That job saved my life! My father was in Campbeltown doing his bit in the Home Guard. The sirens had sounded before and nothing ever happened – just a routine exercise. However, before many minutes passed we knew that this one was different! The buildings shook, the windows rattled and things fell from the wall. My mother decided we must move out.

We gathered our gas masks and dressed warmly. Mum carried her wee tin case containing documents: birth lines, policies and the family photographs. We made our way to the close where the neighbours had all gathered. We prayed the Rosary – how we prayed! By this time the noise was ferocious – shattering glass, crumbling of baffle walls as they collapsed, incendiary bombs and the screech of ambulances as they went up and down the town. The last thing I remember was my mother tucking me up in a blanket in a corner of the close. 'School for you tomorrow and no being late either,' she said. That was the last time I saw her.

I woke up! I thought I was in bed. I tried to turn on my other side. 'The clothes are awful tight,' I thought. I pulled again and discovered that my hands were full of stones – hot ones at that.

I shouted for my mother. No answer. The place was perfectly silent. I shouted again and again and at last I heard my sister Lily answering me. She was underneath me! I felt her head. We were both trapped. Lily urged me to shout and shout. I was falling into unconsciousness. After what seemed like an eternity, I heard Joe's voice. The Bank Cinema was only a few hundred yards away and he had seen the landmine fall on Napier Street. I thought I was safe and lay back waiting to be rescued. This was not to be so easy. My left leg was trapped under one of the steel girders that reinforced the tenement buildings during the war. Moreover the building was on fire, so they couldn't get down to me. I remember being doused by water – by Joe using a stirrup pump. That managed to waken me a bit! I learned later that each rope they put down burned in front of them. I heard the men shouting to each other trying to find a way down. And I overheard Father White and another man talking. 'We can't get her out without injuring her legs, Father.'

He replied, 'We'll have to take her out without her legs, otherwise she'll burn to death.'

Well! That wakened me all right! How could I play hockey, tennis, rounders without legs?

I shot into action! I tore at the rubble trying to loosen myself, and I was encouraged by the men above. I worked fiercely at it and at last Mr McFadden managed to get down, tie a rope all round me and go back up to pull with the others. I pushed and pushed and, at last, with one almighty pull, I found myself dangling in the air! I was soon in the arms of Father White who told me that Lily would be rescued easily now – I had been blocking her way.

The pavement seemed to be a long way down. A soldier was walking along (I would love to know who he was). He called to Father White: 'I'll take her, Father'. Father White was unsure how to get me down.

'I'll jump, Father,' I said. By this time I didn't care – I just wanted away. I took one leap and was caught at the bottom by the soldier. We both laughed. I was safe at last!

I was taken to the Rest Centre in Elgin Street School and wrapped in a blanket. I'll never forget that Rest Centre till the day I die. Some people were crying quietly, some screaming with pain and others just sitting there stupefied. My godmother, Annie Kirk, who owned the sweetie shop at

Napier Street corner was there. Father White spoke to her and she drew back her blanket. Her arm was severed above the elbow. I'll always hear her screams of pain and then the silence when she died. It was my first meeting with death.

Next I was carried through the street on a stretcher. Crowds of people seemed to be there looking for their families and friends. It was Friday. I arrived in Our Holy Redeemer's school – into the hall of the Infant building. Familiar faces at last – Miss Keane, Big Ben Kelly and others. Miss Keane dressed me in one of her very own night dresses and bed jacket. Mauve, I think it was. Was I proud! I kept the jacket for years! It was there that it was discovered I had head injuries as well as leg injuries and would have to go to hospital on Saturday.

On Friday night Mrs McShera took Lily and me home with her to Barns Street. There was another raid! We went into her Anderson shelter and emerged in the morning to more destruction. Windows were broken and the building badly shaken. But no lives were lost.

On Saturday, I was taken to the Royal Infirmary, put into a woman's ward and, I put this on record, I was really well looked after – by doctors and nurses and patients. In fact, I was spoiled!

From time to time, I asked about the rest of my family. I knew Dad, Lily and Joe were all right, but what about Mum, Hugh and Mary? I got no immediate answer, and I knew then that something was badly wrong.

After about three weeks, Father White came to see me. He told me that Mum, Hugh and Mary had been killed and had been buried from Our Holy Redeemer's, and were laid to rest in Dalnottar Cemetery,

Our home was gone, so where would the rest of us live?

St Margaret's School was a boarding school for girls at that time. It was decided I would be well looked after there, so I agreed to go. By the way, the night I arrived in Paisley there was another air raid. Paisley was badly hit – one of our gym teachers was killed. I began to think Hitler was after me personally!

However, with the nuns' loving care, I learned to use my leg again and was soon playing rounders and hockey and climbing trees. Lily and Joe lived in digs and in time married. The worst effect, to my mind, was the break up of the family. It was 1953 before I came back to Clydebank.

All the 'getting to know you' years were gone and we had to get to know each other again.

My only reminder of childhood days is my mother's purse, disintegrating each year, with its contents – the medal of St Theresa and the key of our piano, and the contents of that wee tin case my mother took to the close. Many a time I enjoy looking at all the photographs, some badly water-marked. They remind me of my happy childhood spent in Napier Street.

Kathleen McConnell's mother, Mary Kate McConnell

Anne Harvie

I'M HOME SAFE, MUM

On March 14th 1941, my brother aged fifteen, was at a Boys' Brigade meeting in a church hall in Renfrew. When the sirens sounded, he went with his friend to his house nearby. But he wanted to get home as he knew my mother would be worrying about him and no amount of persuasion by his friend's mum to stay until the raid was over could stop him.

How he managed to reach home we will never know, but make it he did, and his last words to my mother were, 'I'm home safe, Mum.' He stayed at the front of the close while the rest of us were at the back. It seemed like only minutes later we could hear this awful whistling noise, then silence before an almighty bang as the front of the close received a direct hit.

My brother Alex Ross died with at least eight of our neighbours that night. He was the only son in the middle of four sisters, and we have only one photograph of the five of us as we lost everything that dreadful night.

Margaret James

LA SCALA

On the evening of Thursday, 13th March, 1941, I took a half crown from my handbag, waved a cheery farewell to my parents and set off from my home at 55 Granville Street to walk to the dancing at the 'Wedderlea.'

On that evening, no pencil torch was required to guide my footsteps in the blackout for it was a beautiful, clear full moon and the town was clearly defined as though in broad daylight. At the entrance to the dance hall, I paused, looked across the narrow street at the 'La Scala' picture house and, on impulse, changed my mind about attending the dancing. The 'La Scala' was a huge, white-painted building standing on a hill and, like the nearby Singer's factory clock, was a landmark which could be seen from many miles distant.

As I entered the picture house, I little realised that I was seeing the Clydebank I knew and loved for the last time, for within an hour, most of the town would be one huge fireball.

At precisely 9 p.m., the proprietors of the picture house announced that the air raid sirens had sounded. At first everyone remained seated, since we were well used with the sound of air raid sirens. We were soon disturbed, however, and we could clearly hear and indeed feel that bombs were being dropped on the town and in very close proximity. The management instructed patrons to move back from the front of the picture house and take shelter under the balcony, which we did. In the meantime, the film continued and this state of affairs persisted until the operator was forced to leave his post because of shrapnel. The management announced that a landmine had fallen on Kilbowie Hill, causing severe damage and bursting the main water main as a result. They requested that we remain in our present position and be watchful for incendiaries entering the building via the roof.

A little more than two hours had passed before several of the audience including myself went to the open side door of the building and looked out towards the four storey tenement about fifty yards away. This building, which ran the full length of Kilbowie hill, was blazing from end to end. It was a sight I shall never forget and it completely obliterated any further view of the town.

Around midnight, walking casualties began to come into the foyer and we ran to help them, administering first aid as best we could, using strips torn from undergarments and even handkerchiefs as emergency slings. Everything was done to assist the slightly wounded at the picture house, but seriously injured people were removed as quickly as possible to the first aid posts. I learned very early on that the 'Wedderlea' Dance Hall had sustained a direct hit and that approximately thirty six people had been killed.

I was aware that my parents would have reported for duty at the sound of the sirens – my mother to the first aid post and my father for duty as a Special Constable. So I had no further knowledge of them, nor they of me. All I could do was to wait and hope and say a silent prayer for their safety.

It was a long night during which we were subjected to prolonged bombardment but miraculously the picture house did not sustain a direct hit. The All Clear sounded at 6.30 a.m. and, shortly afterwards, my father arrived, looking for me. They had heard about the 'Wedderlea' sustaining a direct hit and their alarm was only dispelled when my father found me at the 'La Scala', the only building still standing in the area.

Nothing could have prepared me for the shock created by the sight of the devastation wrought upon the town of Clydebank in such a brief period of time. I can only liken it to my idea of what a glimpse into 'Dante's Inferno' would be like. Dazed and severely shocked, my dad and I began to try to make our way towards our home in Granville Street. We climbed over huge building slabs and mountains of rubble and eventually arrived at what had formerly been Granville Street. We were relieved to see my mother standing with a number of our old neighbours on what was left of our home. It was just a heap of rubble and it was obvious that all we had was what we stood up in. We were pleased to be alive and together and the moment was precious.

We decided to try and make our way to Bannerman Street, within a short distance, where my mother's brother and sister lived. Another brother of my mum's lived on Kilbowie Hill which was on our route, but, since their home had been badly damaged by fire, we had no way of knowing their whereabouts. In fact, it was many weeks before we learned that they had survived and were living in Greenock.

At Bannerman Street, we found my aunts and uncles safe and well, but, like us, their homes had been destroyed and they also had just what they stood up in.

With great difficulty we made our way to Janetta Street School where buses were to be provided to evacuate survivors. People formed into a queue four or five deep and seemingly endless. We stood all day waiting for buses which did not arrive, during which time we were served with one bowl of soup, handed out by one of the voluntary organisations. In hindsight the prospect of evacuation by bus was unreal because there was no way they could possibly make their way into the town or out of it.

At 8 p.m. it became imperative that we find some form of shelter as quickly as possible. We made our way to Thomson Street, about half a mile away, and there found a surface air raid shelter into which we hurried, thankful to be under cover. The number of people in the shelter was about twenty, and it was not long before one of them went over to a notice posted at the entrance. It read 'Danger – Unexploded Bomb.' so our feeling of thankfulness was shortlived. and we had to get up and go.

The sirens had sounded at 8.30 p.m. and it was essential to find cover as soon as possible. We hurried on, as heavy bombs started to fall, and after half a mile or so, we found a shelter that was empty. As we entered the shelter, I saw a minister from the manse across the road ushering his family into a private car. I do not know whether they managed to get out of the town, but I do know that his manse received a direct hit during the course of the night and was completely destroyed. The shelter took the full force of the shock wave caused by the impact and, for what seemed like a period of minutes, shook like a trampoline.

At no time, did I encounter any panic or hysterics. The people about me were dazed and shocked by it all and we clung to each other, talking quietly but at the same time trying to drown out the horrible screaming sound of the bombs. It is a sound that will remain with me forever.

I recall that when we left the shelter shortly after 6 a.m., the sun seemed very reluctant to rise on us. It was murky and there was destruction everywhere around us. The acrid smell of smoke and cordite was sore on the eyes, nostrils and throat. The town of Clydebank was in a terrible state with hardly a building standing. It was like a ghost town.

After another long wait outside what had been a church at the top of Kilbowie Hill, we finally boarded a bus at 8.30 p.m. on Saturday night and left Clydebank. The most pathetic sight that comes to mind was that of family pets – cats, dogs and birds – all having been rescued by their owners, left tied to the church railings because they were not allowed on the buses.

We had not eaten or slept since Thursday , but we were all past caring, thankful to be alive. At about 1 a.m., we arrived at a school in Mossend, Lanarkshire and the people there, not expecting our arrival, had made no arrangements. There was nothing to eat and no place to rest our weary heads. Food was eventually served to us about 4 a.m., but, by that time, I was asleep on the floor of the assembly hall and did not get any. Later we were given car rugs and put in our various family groups in the classrooms. The people who were handling the reception got themselves organised as the day wore on and we were eventually served with a meal, canteen style, in the assembly hall. Later on, we spent some time going round the local farms, obtaining straw with which to stuff our palliasses and so make sleeping on a wooden floor a little more comfortable.

After four or five days at the school, the people of Mossend found billets for all the evacuees. On the Monday morning, my dad and I decided to make our way back to our place of work in Clydebank. We had to obtain money because all we had was what we had in our pockets at the time of the first air raids. There were no banking facilities available to us in Clydebank and there was no such a machine as a Cash Line in those days.

We waited at the Central Railway Station Bridge in Glasgow and, in due course were able to board one of the open lorries heading for Clydebank as part of the clearing up operations. I was able to attend my place of work at Singer's factory which strangely enough had not sustained damage, so work carried on, although to a lesser extent than formerly. After all, we were producing munitions vital to the war effort. My dad and I were earning again, and were able to use the clearing up lorries to travel to and from our billets in Mossend.

In the meantime, after a period of eight weeks, by running backwards and forwards from Mossend to Clydebank during daylight hours and pestering the Council Housing Department, my mother had managed to obtain accommodation for us in a tenement flat at 28 Radnor Street. We had a roof over our heads in Clydebank, but the accommodation left a lot to be desired. There were holes in the gable, asbestos sheets covered the window spaces and there were mice everywhere. Although we had a home, we had no furniture, carpets, bedding or any of the many things that provide comfort. And we had to put up with the restrictions of wartime rationing. Life was pretty miserable and, at times, uncomfortable.

Of course, there were amusing moments, but most important of all, we were alive and together as a family. For this, we have given thanks many times since. Though we had lost all our belongings and many very sentimental possessions, we were able to rehabilitate ourselves in our own family surroundings. Many, many of our former friends and associates were not so fortunate.

V.M.

SERVANTS' ENTRANCE

At the time of the Blitz, we were just six weeks in our new home in Canberra Avenue. I was eighteen at the time and lived with my widowed mother and my fifteen year old brother Peter.

When the sirens sounded that night, I was up in Millburn Avenue visiting my chum Ina. We sheltered under the big oak table in the dining room. In the morning I made my way down Mill Road and saw the whisky place burning. Further on down at Brown's building, near where the Boilermaker's club is now, all the closes had been bombed and soldiers were busy pulling down dangerous bits of the buildings with big ropes. Just past Castle Square I met my mother, out looking for me. And I saw the soldiers lifting a wee baby out of a damaged building.

My mother had met Bill MacPherson out looking for his wife Cissie. The next day we learnt that she had gone up from Bowling with a present for her sister Jessie's three day old baby. They had gone into a shelter in Pattison Street, and Cissie had been killed. Jessie's eight year old son was killed too. There had been no trace of the baby, but, some days later it was found in a local hospital, unscathed. Bill told my mother that he had found Cissie's body in a pend and that her wedding and engagement rings had been stolen. I know there was some looting after the Blitz. I heard of a man in Clydebank who was sentenced for it.

On Friday morning, my granny, grandpa, aunt and uncle and my brother went away to Helensburgh. My mother and I stayed on. About seven p.m., the army came round and said everyone had to leave Clydebank that night. We stood for a couple of hours up at the Union Church, but the expected buses did not arrive. When the sirens went about nine p.m. we went into the close at the end of Glenruther Terrace and listened to the heavy bombardments. Then incendiaries set the buildings on fire and we had to move along to another close. At two a.m. there was a lull and we went out and we made our way home.

Once there, we only had a break of an hour or so before the sirens started again. The neighbours from upstairs came down and went into our cubby hole under the stairs. There was no room left for any of us to get in. Then a stick of bombs fell right along Canberra Avenue and the blast blew my mother right up the lobby. Across the road, a house was demolished and a wee boy of three was buried under the rubble. He never really recovered from it. It left him mentally impaired.

Next morning when it was light, my mother and I set off for Helensburgh. My mother said, 'You should see your face. It's all black specks!'

'Yours is the same,' I said. It was off the burning oil tanks at Old Kilpatrick.

At Gavinburn, near the bus depot, we hailed an open lorry which had other people in it, and climbed in. It took us as far as Dumbarton and then we had to stand and wait for another lift. Eventually, a big, swanky chauffeur driven car drew up. The gentleman in it asked us where we were going and then gave us a lift to Helensburgh.

All our relatives were in West Kirk Hall and we waited there for our billets. People taking in evacuees received five shillings per evacuee per week. We were taken in, my mother, brother and I, by a Mrs Johnstone from a big house in Upper Helensburgh.

There were only two single beds in our room, so Peter got one and my mother and I had to share the other one. There was a big drive up to the house, and Mrs Johnstone employed a cook (whom my mother called Clara Cluck) and a housemaid (Margaret). I once went up the front drive and got a terrible row from Mrs Johnstone. She said I was always to come in by the servants' entrance. One day, when Mrs Johnstone was out, Margaret took my mother in to see the dining room. It was beautiful, with a big, oval glass table.

A Lt. Commander at Ardencaple Castle (the HQ for the Clyde Naval Base) was billeted at John Logie Baird's father's house, the same house that my Auntie Hannah and her children were sent to. The Lt. Commander sent for the Medical Officer to examine Aunt Hannah's children – in case they were verminous and might infect his children. But Margaret, Mrs Johnstone's housekeeper, heard from the Medical Officer that the Lt. Commander would be lucky if he had such healthy children as Auntie

Hannah had. She had always fed them good, healthy food.

We were still in Helensburgh in May, at the time of the Greenock Blitz. The Germans bombed the ships and Lyle's Sugar. Everything was blazing and could be seen from Mrs Johnstone's house high above Helensburgh. She invited us up to Master Ivor's room for a better view. 'It's a lovely view over Greenock, just like Fairyland,' she said.

Edith Little

THE WEE BLACK BAG

Lying in the wardrobe drawer
With the book for paying the rent
Pulled out with all our valuables
Each time the siren went
The handbag she'd got for a birthday
Along with a bottle of scent......

Time had worn the handles,
But the clasp was firm and good,
The leather unscratched and shiny,
With a frame like polished wood.
Inside lay all the papers
Marriage lines, certificates of birth,
Documents folded up neatly,
All going under the earth.
For whenever that siren sounded,
And to the shelter our feet we did drag
A yell always came from the bedroom,
'Haud on, till I get my wee bag'......

The guns had started to answer,
A warden was doing his nut,
'Come oan missus, ah canny help it,
If the door o' yer wardrobe's got stuck,
An' yer son canny find his troosers,
Bide here, and yer chancin yer luck.'

That all-clear was finally sounded,
We knew it would be the last,
And they would have to start re-building

Homes flattened by bombing and blast,
Their contents had all been scattered,
Stubbed out, like the end of a fag,
I wonder now, did it all really happen,
And where is the wee black bag?

Frances Barclay

THERE'S NO SCHOOL TODAY

My five year old brother was in bed and we were waiting for Dad to come home from working late in Singer Factory. There was a roaring fire going and his meal was almost ready. It was about eight forty five and Mum was telling me to get ready for bed (nine at night was considered bedtime for an eleven year old) when the sirens sounded. We expected this to be one of the usual short raids, so after telling us to put on our siren suits, Mum and my grandfather, who lived with us, decided to wait till Dad came home before going to the shelter in the back garden. But, by the time he arrived, it was too risky to cross the garden, so it was decided we would stay in the small bedroom which, because of the design of the house, had three inside walls and was thought to be the safest place.

Dad only stayed long enough to have something to eat, get his steel helmet, and he was off to the A.R.P. post halfway down Hardgate.

It was a terrifying night. We were lucky we had wooden shutters on all our windows, but Mum and Grandpa had to take turns keeping them closed in case a light should show. By morning all the windows were smashed, slates were off the roof and all the ceilings were damaged. All caused by blast. When we went into the garden, there were quite a few burnt out incendiary bombs. Luckily they had missed the house. One thing I can remember is a school friend coming out of her house yelling, 'There's no school today!'

The second night we went to the shelter when the sirens sounded. We were joined by my aunt, two cousins and an elderly lady from Clydebank who had lost her house the previous night. My brother and cousins were too young to understand what could happen to us, but during the night I began to feel sick. When Dad and another warden appeared to check that we were alright, Mum unearthed a small bottle of whisky, poured a teaspoonful for me and gave Dad the bottle to hold. When she turned to take it back, Dad was sleeping on his feet and the bottle was upside down – empty. How a strict teetotaller explained the smell I'll never know.

He didn't sleep long. A stick of incendiaries landed on the hedge behind our coalshed only yards from the shelter, and both men dived out to extinguish them.

We were lucky the house survived and so did we. There were no official evacuation plans, as Hardgate and Duntocher had not been considered to be in any danger. We had to get away, so Mum and Dad contacted friends in Aberfoyle, who promised to find us accommodation. But we had to get there. A neighbour said he would take us if we could get petrol coupons. A local farmer offered them and my aunt and I were sent to the farm. We took a shortcut over the Knowes, and had only gone about fifty yards when we spotted the tail-fin of a bomb sticking out of the ground. We ran, stopped, spotted another, and arrived at the farm shaking and exhausted. We walked back along Cochno Road – no more shortcuts for us.

We arrived in Aberfoyle and were given a large room in the local tailor's house. The lady of the house insisted we call ourselves 'refugees'; 'evacuees' sounded too common to her. I cannot remember what she charged for the room, but I do know we had to use oil lamps and not electric light.

On Monday the 17th, we were enrolled in the local school, my brother in the infant class, my cousin three classes above and myself in qualifying. It was a shock to the system. I had only been at this level one month and all my new classmates were almost ready to sit the exam in June. However, thanks to a teacher who had been transferred with pupils from Church Street School, Partick, I was able to catch up.

Dad travelled to Aberfoyle almost every weekend, but by June 1942, Mum decided it was time for my brother and herself to go home. It was arranged that I would live in the same house as the Church Street girls. Two sisters – both widows – had the unenviable task of looking after ten teenagers. They were strict but very fair. They must have had many a nightmare – one girl in particular had to be de-loused every time she returned from a visit home. During my stay there, one of the sisters was told that her son was missing in Singapore. She told me years later that it was the girls who kept her going.

I returned home in 1943 and had to go to Dumbarton Academy since

Clydebank High had been destroyed. I was lucky I was able to pick up with my school friends again. Today I still have the same friends and connections from Aberfoyle.

Patricia Drayton

EVACUEES IN HELENSBURGH

Cardross had a few houses quite badly damaged by the blitz, but Helensburgh was really very lucky and did not suffer much at all in that way.

We had a small room under the stairs in the cottage and we had it fitted with seats, rugs, etc, plus some food should the raid last a long time. Some of our neighbours from across the street came to share this shelter with us.

During the Clydebank raid the evacuees poured into the town and the church halls were used to give them shelter until billets could be found for them in the town. I can remember being sent to the old parish church hall with a big basket of pancakes to help feed them and I can still see in my mind's eye those poor, unhappy people and their children who had lost everything.

William K. S. Campbell

CORNED BEEF

The third year pupils were asked to volunteer to help out by giving out rations to the evacuees coming into Helensburgh from Clydebank. We assembled at St Joseph's School at the corner of King Street and James Street. It was my primary school at one time. The benches were erected and each pupil was given an item of rations to give out: powdered milk, powdered eggs, soup and so on. Mine was corned beef (same shape of tin as now). Then the women and kids came in. I think the rations were a can of meat per adult and a can between two kids. There was always some begging for more. It was something you don't forget.

The billeting officers were going around to find accommodation for families and kids. This was where you found out the divisions in Helensburgh between the 'upper class' (above King Street) and the 'lower class' (below King Street). For example, my aunt (with no family) in a kitchen, living room and bedroom took in a woman and two teenagers, while a few of the ones up the 'Hill' needed to keep room for their relations coming from London.

But this was a time when religion never mattered. We were all 'Jock Tamson's Bairns.'

James Bell

LOSS OF A FATHER'S INFLUENCE

My mother, Rosetta Bell (née Parker) was killed in the Blitz. I was aged two and have no recollection of her, no memories, no photographs, nothing that could link her with me.

In the 'The Clydebank Blitz' by I. M. M. McPhail, there is the entry: BELL, Rosetta, age 31. Wife of James G. Bell. 13 March 1941, at 4 Second Terrace.

I understand my Dad was on Warden duty in another area of the town when the tragedy occurred. I and my elder brother Tom, aged 6, were taken, to my aunts in Old Kilpatrick and it was in this loving and caring environment that we were raised. Mitchell Terrace was a red-bricked building of two closes, with eight families in each close. By today's standards, it had vast playing areas, as well as drying greens and a garden for each tenant. These gardens, in most instances perhaps, providing essentials for the family diet. I can remember some kept hens and most had a great variety of vegetables and fruit.

Many happy days were spent there. I only came to the conclusion much later in life that it was an unorthodox family. Perhaps the war made it appear normal. The family was made up of my maiden aunts, Lizzie (our guardian) and Annie, their brother John, cousin Christine (his daughter) and Tom and I. The accommodation was: living room with open range fire, two bedrooms, scullery and outside toilet. We later moved to the luxury of Roman Crescent, Old Kilpatrick.

Into this family group, my dad came mainly on a Friday night to see his two sons. Obviously, from this relatively short time together (and later, after he re-married, a few holidays together) we did not have a definitive father figure, although Uncle John's presence may have compensated in some ways.

My life in Old Kilpatrick was enjoyable and fulfilling. I attended Gavinburn Primary School and Clydebank High School, becoming involved in The Boys' Brigade, an organisation which had an influence throughout my life in so many ways.

Growing up, I gave little thought to the fact that I didn't have parents, a mum and a dad, to discuss day to day trivia and important issues – a family setting similar to my friends. It was not until I was getting married that I began to realise that I had relatives on my mother's side of the family. Indeed, apart from my wedding, no mention was ever made of my mother's family. Consequently, I have even now only one real contact with my mother's side – May Pollock (née Parker) and in recent years we have met, renewed our relationship and reminisced.

I often consider the sacrifice my Aunt Lizzie made to bring two nephews up. She gave up her job as a french polisher. Did she turn down a proposal of marriage? An opportunity to leave the area? Consider also my dad's sacrifice in living a stone's throw away in Clydebank and yet having little or no influence on my upbringing.

My dad was a blacksmith to trade and would tell us stories about his work, and later, he was a teacher of his craft at Stow College and David Dale College, where he was held in high esteem by staff and students. He has been described by many and various people as a gentleman, and this is how I will remember him.

The Clydebank Blitz therefore not only cost me the love of a mother but, through other circumstances, a dad I never really got to know.

Jean Golder

A.R.P. DUTY

In September 1939, I was very ill in the Medical Ward in the Western Infirmary. I remember (after the siren must have gone) the bed being pushed into the centre of the ward, away from the wall, and the mattress, blankets and me being slung under the bed frame.

A year later, having fully recovered, I was doing duty in the A.R.P. in Boquhanran School for three evenings after work, which stopped at 5.30 p.m. The A.R.P. started at 7 o'clock and finished at 11 o'clock, and the police came to escort the girls (as we were then) home.

As time went on, we women had to work night and day shifts. Night shift was 8 p.m. till 8 a.m., day shift 8 a.m. till 5.30 p.m. with three nights late when we worked till 8 p.m. You would think there was no time for any social activities. However, although there was a total blackout, cinemas, dancehalls and theatres were open for entertainment if you cared to take the risk.

This was the pattern of life until the 13th March 1941, the dreadful night Clydebank was blitzed by the German Luftwaffe. I was on night shift and it was the most terrible experience of my life, the planes screaming, bombs exploding and the smell of burning (we learned when the all-clear had been given the whole of the vast wood yard had been burnt to the ground).

When we were allowed to make our way home, tears were streaming down our faces as we looked towards what had been terraced houses on the hill. There was nothing left but huge piles of rubble of what we called the 'Holy City.' It was a nightmare, trying to make your way home, using a detour over roads that were full of holes and rubble, worrying about what you would find when you arrived.

For me, everyone was safe. I was also one of the lucky ones. If I had not been on night shift when the A.R.P. school was bombed and flattened, I would have been on duty at the post. Some of my friends were killed.

The house was declared unsafe, so we were evacuated to Hamilton and had to travel to and from there to our workplace in Clydebank, which added almost four hours on to a twelve hour shift.

Richard Bluer

STEEL SHELTER

I was born in a steel house in MacGregor Street, Clydebank (a sort of post 1914/18 prefab) on 30th March 1930. My parents had moved to Clydebank from the east end of Glasgow so that my father could be nearer to his work. He was employed as Chief Clerk to the Mechanical Engineer's Department of the Clyde Navigation Trust in Renfrew. Some time after I was born we moved to Parkhall, 9 Parkhall Terrace in fact, overlooking the Boulevard and Duntocher. The significance of my father's occupation will appear later in this story.

At the age of five years I attended Boquhanran Primary School until it was closed shortly after the declaration of war. The authorities clearly took the danger of air-raids very seriously then. For a few months, my education ceased and I seem to recall a kind of extended summer holiday beyond September of 1940. Eventually, my parents heard of a schoolteacher also affected by the closure of a school, who was doing private tuition, so for a couple of mornings each week I attended his house in Dalmuir. This ceased when I was then permitted to attend Duntocher Primary School.

The Government issued air-raid shelters (the famous Anderson shelter) to the people, but not to all the people. I guess my father's income exceeded the level for the first issue of shelters. He was concerned about this and arranged to have his own air-raid shelter built – by the Clyde Navigation trust! Built of curved sheet steel, it was bolted into place in its hole in the back garden complete with an emergency rear exit – a hinged overhead door at the rear. It also had an entrance door, floorboards and bench seating round the sides. It was furnished with carpets and cushions for comfort. When the sand bag baffle wall was added to the front, the top earthed and turfed, we were ready for any event – we hoped much better than an Anderson shelter!

Radnor Park School had now been completed or, at least, sufficiently completed to be used and I was transferred there from Duntocher. This probably was early in 1941. My father was one of two car owners in Parkhall Terrace – he had a Standard 10, but he only drove it Spring and Summer. He laid it up during the winter at a large garage area in Duntocher. Yes, he had quite a walk there and back each time he wanted the car and he didn't drive it at night either.

I should also mention that my father, a keen gardener, had a green house which caused considerable amusement with friends and neighbours because of its many loose panes of glass. I doubt if any were securely fixed. The putty had all disintegrated.

My mother was a Director of Clydebank Co-operative Society and had attended a Director's meeting on the evening of the Blitz, but had travelled home by tram car (my parents avoided buses wherever possible) arriving just before the first air-raid sirens went off.

When the warning sounded, the three of us retreated to our shelter. We had used it a couple of times before during brief attacks, but none of these events were as long or as horrific as the one now experienced. Explosions and crashes, both distant and near continued for hours. Occasionally the earth would shake. Our personal experience centred on the following three events.

Huddled as I was in the blankets and pillows, I looked up and noticed that the rear of our shelter, where the emergency exit was, was glowing from red to white with heat, An incendiary bomb had fallen under the flap extending beyond the shelter and had rested on the door. So much for an emergency exit! We left through the front door and scrambled into the house and proceeded to the officially recommended safety area – under the stairs. In the process of this short flight, the scene of desolation in what was familiar surroundings shocked my young mind. Really, all that had happened was that the window casements had been completely blown in, leaving glass fragments and dust everywhere. After a period under the stairs, my father deemed it advisable to return to the shelter.

A few doors along Parkhall Terrace, a couple of brothers, early twenties perhaps (seemed old to me) were watching the display from their Anderson shelter doorway and came urgently to our shelter to tell us that they had seen an incendiary bomb strike our house roof. My father then returned to the house, collected his stirrup pump and bucket, and climbed up into the loft. Incendiary bombs were supposed to be sprayed with water with great caution as direct spraying would cause them to explode. (I'm sure many methods of dousing them were discovered that night!) As my father gently sprayed the bomb, it fell through the attic floor. He collected the equipment and rushed back downstairs into the main bedroom where the bomb was lying on his bed – extinguished.

Another incendiary later landed on our back garden – between the shelter and the house. This time my father tackled it with a spade – he dug up part of the green and covered the bomb with earth! And so we survived the night.

After the all-clear sounded we went to the front of the house and I vividly remember the awesome sight of Duntocher ablaze.

Daylight revealed some of the damage in our locality. The large four-in-a-block at the rear of our house (in Maple Drive ?) wasn't there any more. A large landmine crater covered a large part of the field beyond Parkhall Terrace. Shrapnel (which had been eagerly collected by us kids before) lay everywhere. An amazing puzzle also arose. What had happened to our bin lid? Our next door neighbour (a Mr Conde) supplied the answer. He had come round to see us during a lull in the bombing and found an incendiary burning at the side of the house. He picked up the bin lid and put it over the fire! Another surprise or perhaps not – the greenhouse survived with all its panes intact.

It was a fine sunny day and at first, it was our intention to stay even though we believed that the German bombers would return for a second bombardment. But my resolve, along with my mother's, began to wane as we experienced occasional explosions during the day presumably caused by the detonation of unexploded bombs. By early afternoon, my father walked to Duntocher, retrieved his car, unscathed, and drove us to my mother's cousin in Thornliebank.

The bombers, of course did return and number 9 Parkhall Terrace was struck again by an incendiary bomb. It hit the roof at an angle, plunged through into the bathroom, landed in the wash-hand basin and burned itself out – and so Parkhall Terrace survived as it does to this day.

A few weeks after our flight to Thornliebank, Clydebank Town Council contacted my parents and gave them, I think, three weeks to return or the tenancy would be cancelled. We returned to view our house. All that had been done to make it habitable was that the casement windows had been boarded up wedged back into position. My folks did not find this acceptable, and neither did most other people, so the Council relented this severe attitude with more remedial work. But my parents had already surrendered their base. We lived for approximately twelve months at Thornliebank and then my parents bought a house in Paisley (to be nearer my father's work).

My mother believed for many years that she would return to Clydebank and I remember long journeys by tram car for occasional shopping trips – but we never did return.

Anne S. Newcome (née Reekie)

THE NIGHT OF THE STORK

I was almost six years old when the Second World War began and, although I do not hail from Clydebank, my father had a huge number of cousins in Clydebank, being a cousin of the Ballantyne family who owned the barber's shop. I may say that the Ballantyne family of Clydebank was a big one, to say the least.

I remember the night of the Clydebank Blitz, although I was only about seven or eight years of age. I can remember my father pointing in the direction of Clydebank and seeing the light of the fires reflected in the sky.

Just after the Blitz, I arrived at my grandmother's house in Dumbarton to find it bulging at the seams with relatives from Clydebank who owned no more than the clothes they were wearing.

My father rushed back to our home in Latta street, Dumbarton, and returned with some clothes. There was one cousin who was so shocked that he was in a complete daze, being unable to speak or respond to anyone. My father kitted him out with a complete suit of clothes but still there was no response. He then folded a handkerchief and put it into the breast pocket of his suit, at which point his cousin came to life and ran about, laughing, crying and shouting, 'He's even given me a handkerchief.'

I also remember being taken by my grandmother to visit a great aunt who lived in what she called 'the Holy City.' This area was to the left of Kilbowie Road, going up towards Hardgate. I can still remember the dreadful heaps of debris everywhere and the eerie feeling.

But there was a slightly humorous side to something that happened on the night of the Clydebank Blitz. I was an only child and asked Santa for a little brother or sister each Christmas. While we were in the air raid shelter, the lady who lived above us gave birth to a baby boy. My father, rather unwisely, told me that if we had not been in the shelter, the stork would have stopped at our house! The lady had apparently been given the choice of moving down to the ground floor flat but decided that she would rather 'go down with the building than have the building come down on top of her.'

Emilia Garland

FISH AND CHIP SHOP

My father Val Occardi had a fish and chip shop in Second Avenue up in the 'Holy City', as it was known then. We had moved from Stirling about a year before, and me and my twin sister were very unhappy. We loved Stirling, our home town.

This particular night, the siren sounded and before you could blink, all hell was let loose. I was in the shop on my own. I looked out and Second Avenue was ablaze with incendiaries. I was in shock. I didn't know what to do – here was I sixteen years old and all alone. My dad had gone over to the La Scala for a rest, as Wednesday night in the chip shop was usually a very quiet one. All of a sudden I realised that no-one would be coming in for any fish and chips, so I put the chip pan fire out. An ARP man told me to get to the nearest shelter, but I couldn't leave thinking my dad would appear at any moment! Then I heard that the cinemagoers were not allowed to leave the cinema. An hour later it was decided to turn the cinema into a First Aid Post. Dad arrived and the minute he put his foot in the doorstep, an incendiary fell within a yard. Fortunately a sandbag was close by, and he was able to put it out.

Now it was far too late to find a shelter, so we had to go and sit in the close next to us, and were joined by some of the tenants from the flats above. By now it was around midnight. We heard this whistling bomb come down and then the building just shook and shook. We were all too dumbfounded to speak. We knew that the bomb was very nearby but we had to stay put, we had no option. At eight a.m. the all clear went. We left the close and saw buildings demolished, some still on fire. How we were spared I shall never know.

The ARP were in full swing looking for that 'whistling bomb'. My dad told me to make for home where my mum and twin sister were. He wanted to board up his broken windows! As they lived in Coatbridge, I realised I was in for a long walk. Oh the devastation all around! Folk were in a daze, looking for their families. I walked and walked and as I walked along the main road, I came upon a house which had taken a direct hit, and realised I knew the family who lived in it. The priest was standing on top of the rubble with the firefighters looking for bodies. This was the Docherty family who used to come into our shop. They were super people. The father and six of their children were killed. The mother was injured but survived to give birth to a daughter. It all seems so stupid. All these innocent people. They didn't deserve this.

I don't recall how far I must have walked before I found a tram car to take me to Coatbridge. It was noon by then. I remember it as if it was yesterday. It was tears all round. My mum and I and Marie (my twin sister) just hugged and hugged.

It was hours before Dad came home. He had managed to board up the windows, but just as he finished the job, the ARP told him that they had found the whistling bomb – it was right next door in the paper shop. Even now I shudder at the thought of what might have been, but for some reason the folks in that building were spared to live another day. Naturally our shop was blown up by the ARP lads – so much for Dad's efforts.

About six years ago I visited Clydebank, where my mother eventually moved, and when I wandered down to Second Avenue, I was quite surprised to see that where our shop was is just a pile of grass, even though there are new houses built all along the road. I cannot fathom that one out!

Nanette Forsyth

THROUGH THE GOLF COURSE

The morning after the first night of the Blitz, my parents and I set off for Mountblow to find out how my grandmother had fared. We walked down the Soo's Back through Dalmuir Golf Course, moving quietly as there were unexploded parachute mines on either side. On the grass near the mines, lay burnt out incendiary bombs. A sticky substance which had oozed out of the bomb cases gave off a nauseating smell. We were glad to reach Mountblow and relieved that my grandmother was well and that her house had suffered only minor damage.

Having decided to leave the town after the second night, we walked to Kilbowie Road only to find it closed. In the middle of the hill, just below Graham Avenue, water from burst mains was shooting up into the air and rushing downhill. At the junction with Montrose Street, A.R.P. Wardens were directing people towards roads that were passable. Turning back, we made our way through Parkhall to the Boulevard, where we waited at the Tomato Farm (now the site of the West Highway Hotel) until a passing motorist stopped and gave us a lift to Milngavie.

Tom Hunter

KILPATRICK HILLS

Throughout the day and late into the evening, people passed our house wheeling barrows, perambulators and all kinds of strange vehicles piled to overflowing with perhaps their sole remaining belongings. They were making for the Kilpatrick Hills, which lie at this part above the Clyde, in order to encamp there. Hundreds of these unfortunate people must have passed and it reminded me of 'The Great Trek' in history when the Boers were forced to leave their homes. That night the bombers came again!

Ellen Cunningham

THE BOWLING GREEN

My mother Ellen Timney and her family were blitzed out of Livingstone Street and evacuated to Wishaw. My mother stayed in Wishaw in her billet for about a year, while my father travelled each day from Wishaw to the shipyard in Greenock. There were no shelters built when Livingstone Street was bombed. The standard practice was for all the tenants to shelter in the downstairs flat, if caught by the siren. Or to go to the bowling green and spread their bedding there if they could get out in time. The area was an enemy target because the Singer factory nearby was making rifles.

James Wotherspoon

AIR-RAID SHELTERS

The thirteenth of March 1941 for me started as a routine working day in the Tool and Cutter department in Singer's. What makes it stand out in my memory was that I had an addition to my work force, a young man about thirty, a refugee from the bombing in London. He told me some harrowing details of his experiences of the London Blitz and the carnage which one parachute bomb would cause.

On occasions prior to the Blitz we would be wakened during the night by the sirens and hear the menacing tone of the German bombers, not the regular hum of the British planes, but two tones with about a semi-tone in between. But no bombs were dropped here. I can remember one such night. I believe it would be the early hours of Saturday the twenty sixth of July nineteenth forty, and no bombs were dropped. But next day we were at Helensburgh and we saw a Clyde tug which had a huge electric coil on her deck projecting about two feet over the side. It was patrolling in lanes up and down the Firth to detonate parachute mines which had been dropped there in the early morning raid. The reason I can remember the date was that it was the last day of the holidays and people returning to

Glasgow from Dunoon and Rothesay had to be brought back to Glasgow by bus as the Clyde passenger steamers could not venture on the Firth until it had been cleared of mines.

There was another alert before the Blitz. I cannot recall the precise time. It may have been in November nineteen forty when the Germans came on a reconnaissance raid about 7.30 p.m. and dropped flares for aerial photography, the excellence of which we were able to see after the war. This was a warning which should have made us better prepared.

I usually worked late until 9.00 p.m. But this night I had a night off and at 9.00 p.m. I turned on the radio to hear the news from the B.B.C. Almost at once the alert siren sounded to be followed a few minutes later by the sound of bombs. I immediately escorted my family to the shelter, one at a time, the youngest first. I could hear the whine of the falling bombs and, with each explosion, felt a hot blast on my cheek, but I didn't see the flash of the explosion. This was an introduction to what went on all during the night, with a row of houses to the west of us in flames. The warning whine of the bombs would last four or five seconds, and sometimes the bomb didn't explode. We had our worst experience when the landmine was dropped seemingly on top of us. They were fitted with sound devices like rockets rushing towards you. This lasted about thirty seconds during its fall, getting closer and closer until there was a terrible explosion followed for some time by the debris that had been thrown in the air. The houses closest to the explosion were completely wrecked, the street and surroundings were littered with slates, all the windows were blown in, the complete frames which are embedded in the plaster, all the ceilings had collapsed, and the two skylights in their heavy cast iron frame were torn from the roof and laid about thirty feet from the building with not a pane of glass broken. But, what was important, none of us had a scratch.

However, some of our neighbours had not been so fortunate. One was killed when a wooden door that he had fitted to the shelter doorway was blown in and hit him on the head. I believe there were another ten people in the shelter, who were uninjured. Five more people were killed, two in one shelter and three in the shelter next to them. I saw these shelters about a week later, and they were in a dreadful state. One had the door panel blown right through to the back wall. The other shelter was in a similar state, but the whole shelter was partly blown out of the ground. I feel that if the shelters had been installed with the doors facing the building, the occupants might have survived as there were other shelters equally close, but at right angles and with their doors facing the buildings, and, although there were some injuries in them, there were no fatalities.

There was a pause in the bombing about 3 a.m. and we thought it was over for the night. It was then I learnt my near neighbour, Joe Struthers had been killed. After a pause of about twenty minutes, the bombing re-started and continued until the all clear went about 6 a.m. Then it was not long before the alert sounded again and we had to return to the shelter.

Our home was no longer habitable. A bomb had landed in the middle of the road cutting off water and power supplies, and we couldn't even make a cup of tea. We seemed to have lost all initiative and were feeling demoralised. Then my sister, who was a sister in Erskine Hospital and had witnessed the night's carnage, appeared on the scene and got us all organised.

E.L.

THE LAST METER WAS MORE FULL

At the beginning of the incendiary raids on the first night of the Blitz, my father and brother and other neighbours carried out their furniture and stacked it on the pavement at the Agamemnon plots. On the Friday morning, since no damage had been done to their houses, they put all the furniture back. That night, bombs demolished our closes and everything was lost.

On the second night of the Blitz, my mother stood in the lobby, wearing her hat as she always did and carrying her corsets under her arm! We went to my gran's house – it was never bombed- and it was there all our arrangements for departure were made. My father and mother went to Dundee to my Uncle Samuel's. I stayed with my two sons, aged seven and five, at Gran's house. We eventually went to stay with my husband's uncle in Balornock, and he and I travelled to work every day, to Singer's where we both worked. My gran, being a pensioner, was taken away with others and put into Dumbarton Poorhouse. She told my mother, 'Kate, get me out of here.'

My sister-in-law's sister, her husband and child were killed in the Blitz. I accompanied my sister-in-law to identify the bodies at St. James' Church. They just looked as if they were lying sleeping – not a blemish on them. They were killed by the blast.

A week or so after the Blitz, I went up after work to Gran's – the house was empty apart from me – to get a change of clothing before travelling back to Balornock. By the time I was ready to leave, I realised I was too late to catch a bus, so, fully clothed, I just lay down on the bed, under the quilt. Although most people had left Clydebank, there seemed to be lots of tramping about on the stairs. Suddenly the door burst open and three or four men came in and emptied the meter. As I cooried down under the quilt, I heard them say, 'The last meter was more full.'

I went to the town hall to negotiate getting my two boys evacuated. Gran Craig spoke to Dr Strang and he got me a very good billet for the boys. It was in Ayrshire between Moscow and Kilmarnock, a wee farm called 'Tawthorn Smiddy'. The boys stayed there from 1941 to 1943 and I went down to visit them every weekend. They were very happy there, and the farming family, also the Craigs, were very good to them.

Back in Clydebank, some five or six years after the Blitz, my two sons, although given strict instructions not to, used to play in the shell of the Benbow Hotel. One day my son told me, 'Drew and I were climbing in the Benbow and saw skeletons there.' I felt I had to report it to the police, so I went along for constable Kenny McLee, who lived near us. He said he'd have to investigate and the result was that three or four skeletons were discovered – men who had been burned during the Blitz.

Sarah Hughes

HELD BY THE HAIR

When the bombing started, I was at home with my mother and two older brothers in the bottom flat at 20 Bannerman Street. My father was at work in Singer's factory. All the neighbours came down to our house and the door was tied. I remember all the windows came in and the building went on fire, but, for me at the age of seven, the worst thing was the noise of the guns and the whistling bombs.

We wandered about trying to get into shelters. My mother, who was expecting a baby, had no shoes, and she held me by the hair so that I wouldn't get lost. Eventually, we did get into a shelter in Montrose Street and stayed there until morning. Then we found my father and my brothers and went to my aunt's house. Later we went up on to the boulevard to lie flat in the fields.

We were taken first to Helensburgh. As we travelled, shrapnel was hitting the bus and my mother was hysterical. When we got there, we were directed to St Joseph's Hall where we were given a camp bed and some clothes. Afterwards, we were evacuated to Craigendoran. It was difficult because nobody wanted a baby and three other children. But eventually, we were placed in a house called Dunvegan, in Campbell Street. We stayed there for four years and I went to St Joseph's Primary School.

Jessie Grieve Gow

I THOUGHT YOU WERE DEAD

In 1941, I lived at number 23 Parkhall Terrace, Dalmuir. It was a quiet cul-de-sac terrace of about twenty families, with houses on one side only, and an open view down a large field to the Boulevard from Glasgow to Dumbarton, and the Kilpatrick Hills beyond.

We lived in an upstairs house of a four in a block. Our house was situated about half way along the terrace. From our living room windows, we had a magnificent view right down the Clyde Estuary to the hills beyond the Holy Loch, about twenty miles distant as the crow flies.

Our neighbours were: through the wall at number 25, the Millar family, David and Jean with son David; below us, at number twenty one, the Harvie family, Walter, Tamar and twins, also named Walter and Tamar; at number twenty seven, the Moore family, Albert and Elsie, who were wardens, and Phyllis, their only surviving daughter.

Thursday 13 March 1941 was a lovely, cold, bright day. In the afternoon, I went to a shop in Kilbowie Road, which had a small lending library. (2d per book per week). As I entered the shop, the owner of the library was telling a commercial traveller that, if the blitz ever came, his shop would be safe; they would only bomb the main street (about a mile away, downhill) where John Brown's shipyard was situated. That very night, along with many houses and shops in Kilbowie Road, the lending library received a direct hit. As the owner's house was above the shop, he lost everything.

That evening, my friend Bunty Rennie and I were having our supper, a great treat of ham and egg. (Because of food rationing, we got one egg a week if we were lucky). Bunty, a friend from my girlhood days in Girvan, used to visit me weekly. On account of the blackout, she would stay overnight, as it was not a good idea to be a lone woman travelling at night during the blackout.

I put the wireless on to hear the Nine O'clock News. The news had just started when, through it, we heard the air raid siren. We roused Sheila, aged 8, dressed her, and grabbed a small case with insurance papers, money, etc. in it. As we left the house, Bunty lifted a travelling rug from the settee, saying, 'this might be the Blitz.' (By 1941, we really thought that the Blitz would never come.) We went along Parkhall Terrace to number 15, and to the shelter of Mr and Mrs Tidje. The Tidjes did not like to be in the shelter alone during air raid alerts and had previously asked us to join them when an alert came.

The Tidjes' shelter, unlike the usual steel Anderson shelter, was made of railway sleepers, and had over 200 sandbags on top. It also had heat and light. Early in the raid, a blast from a nearby bomb lifted all 200 sandbags off the roof of the shelter, and we could see moonlight through the cracks in the sleepers. There was no more heat or light after that.

The bombs soon started to fall, very near. We sat and listened to them screaming down and wondered when our turn would come. A block of houses in the next road was on fire – we heard the tins in the cupboards exploding with the heat. It was only a few yards away. Every time I heard a bomb coming, I covered Sheila's head with the travelling rug.

We heard the wardens saying that a stick of bombs had flattened Oak road (a road round the corner from us). Another house, very near to us, got a direct hit, and a landmine fell on its shelter. The mother and daughter of twelve were killed. I had seen the little girl out playing on her bike earlier that day.

The anti-aircraft guns up in the Kilpatrick Hills fired for only about an hour. It was about two miles away as the crow flies, and we could hear the orders to fire quite clearly. "Fire number one" – BOOM – "Number one has fired, sir." The guns were knocked out after only one firing. The long hours passed until, at six in the morning, we heard the All Clear sounding, and came out of the shelter.

Strangely, never during the raid did I feel any fear. My only thought was that, if we were hit, we would all go and not be left maimed. Also, although we were in the shelter for nine hours, we never even thought about needing the bathroom! We talked about every subject except the hell that was going on round about us. Mercifully, Sheila slept through most of the Blitz and my friend Bunty, normally a nervous person, was marvellous – she did not flinch once.

When we came out, we picked our way along the terrace to our house. What a sight! The front door was blasted open. Inside, broken glass was all over the staircase and the floors, and there was a very strange smell through the house. I discovered that the bathroom cabinet had been blasted off the wall and, lying in the wash basin, was a broken bottle of 'Sloan's Liniment', hence the odd smell. All the windows were broken. In the big bedroom, the dressing table had been blown on top of the bed. The wooden frames of the bedroom windows were inside the room, leaving the raw brickwork showing. The window and its frame in Sheila's room were hanging out, held only by the window cords. In the living room, the windows were also blown in and, on the table, there was a piece of bomb casing, about three inches by one inch in size, quarter of an inch thick, jagged and sharp. There was neither water nor electricity, so, being all electric, the house was not habitable. The field in front of the house contained about twelve unexploded landmines, so we were ordered to leave the area.

Bunty's brother, David Rennie, came up to Parkhall Terrace to see whether we had survived. Although his home was in Girvan, he was employed in war work in Dalmuir at the Royal Ordnance factory. He arrived in a dishevelled state. The factory had been hit, and he lost all his gear, money and his jacket. He also had seen some of his workmates killed beside him.

Bunty set off separately to try to get to her job at Wendy's Tearoom in Sauchiehall Street in Glasgow. She had to obtain a lift and, when she arrived at Wendy's, her face was black and streaked with smoke. Sheila and I set off across the Great Western Road Boulevard to the nearby village of Duntocher. We must have been some sight, with our dirty faces and tangled hair! As we walked, I was struck by the terrible smell of burning – the whole town seemed to be ablaze.

We contacted a friend, Alice MacNab, to check that Sheila's younger sister, Catherine Gow, who was being looked after by Alice was alright. When Alice saw us, she broke down. 'I thought that Parkhall was all gone, and that you were all killed,' she said Alice told me that, in Duntocher, in one house which had been bombed, a woman had been separated from her little boy by rubble, but she managed to hold on to his hand all night, only to find in the morning that he was dead.

When we got to the tram terminus at Duntocher, we saw a double-decker bus lying in a bomb crater, and a tramcar upended. At this point, there was a warning, and we all dived into the shelter at the tram terminus. It was only the Germans back over again photographing. The warden at the shelter asked us where we were going and flagged down a passing car. He told the driver, 'Take the lady and the little girl to Anniesland.'

When we arrived at my mother's house, at 11 Rippon Drive, she burst into tears. This was most unlike her for she was a stern woman and I had never before seen her weep. She said, 'I thought you were dead.'

It transpired that a friend of her son-in-law, a fellow lawyer, had passed by Parkhall on the Great Western Boulevard on his way into Glasgow. He had thought that Parkhall Terrace had been bombed to the ground, and had telephoned my brother-in-law, who had told my mother to face the near certainty that we were all dead.

H. C.

DID YOU GET MY DANCE FROCK?

Our house in Duntocher was where the Antonine Centre is now. That first night of the Blitz, my mother and father and I and wee dog called Rover (he was just a wee cairn terrier) sat in the house for about an hour, until things began to get worse. Then we went into the Anderson shelter. When we got there, my mother remembered she had not brought the wee tin with the policies, etc. So I ran back and got it. I was twenty one at the time.

Suddenly there was a shuddering thud, and it was our house which had been hit – just a few feet from us. It was a landmine, as I understand. We went up to the public shelter on the main road. There were about fifty people in it.

My sisters, Mary (19) and Betty (23) were both elsewhere. Mary had been at a dance, so she spent the night at a friend's shelter in Dalmuir. When she arrived home and saw the state of our house, she started to cry, thinking we had got bombed. Betty had stayed on with her future mother-in-law in Dumbarton. When I told her what had happened, she responded with, 'Did you get my dance frock?' She had just got a lovely dress for the office dance.

On the Friday morning, my mother, father, Mary and I got a lift in one of the firm's lorries to Neilston where my mother came from. The second night of the Blitz, our house was flattened and we lost everything.

My mother and father and I stayed with my aunt. My mother and father had the kitchen, and my aunt and I shared the bed settee. My young sister stayed with a cousin of my mother's. They were early bedders and, when she used to come in at 10 p.m., she'd find they were in bed and had left her a glass of milk. So Mary finally rebelled and joined us downstairs where we were staying.

Some friends, of course, never survived the Blitz. There was one friend of mine, a girl called Elizabeth Campbell. I used to meet her at night school before the war. She was quite left wing in her views, whereas some of us liked the Royal Family. Elizabeth volunteered for A.R.P. duties and used to chide us for not doing likewise, since we were so much for King and Country. Their house got a direct hit at the triangle at Hawthorn Street, and their mother and the three girls were killed. Their father found this out when he got home from Brown's night shift.

Helen Beattie

WHAT SHOULD I DO WITH THIS, BOB?

In Radnor Street, the morning after the first night bombing, some of the incendiaries did not ignite after landing. One of the neighbours carried one down to the A.R.P Warden's post, asking, 'what should I do with this, Bob?' His answer was, 'Just leave it there, and if it's not collected in ten days, you can have it back.'

I remember that the back draught from a big landmine that dropped near our house in Hawthorn Street sucked all the freshly ironed clothes off the kitchen pulley, out of the kitchen window and dear knows where they dropped. Probably somewhere in the High Park!

Ada Hardie

HAWTHORNE STREET SHELTER

On the first night of the blitz, my mother, four sisters and myself sheltered in the cupboard under the stairs. On the second night, she decided we were to shelter in Clydebank High School which was nearby. On the way there, we met neighbours going to the shelter in Hawthorne Street and they asked us to go there too. However, my mother carried on to the school and there we saw lots of bodies.

The next morning we passed the shelter on our way home and found that it had been flattened and everyone in it killed. Our house had been destroyed too.

We walked to the Town Hall and were put on buses to Alexandria where we were billeted in Susannah Street.

Alex Hardie

BENBOW HOTEL

My mother, father, aunt, uncle and I were at the Queen's Theatre in Glasgow and were walking home to Clydebank, sheltering in closes between waves of bombers. The shrapnel was clattering off the roofs and pavements. One bomb came very near. It shook the close and I was blown out. We all kissed each other goodbye.

Later we started out again and when we reached Kingsway, a lady came out and invited us into her house until the morning. When we passed Kilbowie Road, the tramlines were all twisted and pointing skyward. When we saw the Benbow Hotel in the distance, we thought: 'Good, it's still standing,' but when we reached home and looked through the window, we saw it was a shell.

My grandmother was severely injured in the Benbow Hotel and died of her wounds. The next day my grandfather took us to his brother in Greenock. Then we had the Greenock Blitz. We ended up staying with the Gillies family in King Edward Street, next to the Torpedo Works.

Sister Nora H. Foley (from Darien, Connecticut)

163 SECOND AVENUE

We lived at 163 Second Avenue and lost our house in the first fifteen minutes of 13th March. We went to an air-raid shelter in St Stephen's School and after many hours it fell on us. Seven people were killed . My mother, granny and I were buried. My father and another man who offered help, dug us out with their bare hands, my eleven year old brother doing his best to help them. A doctor and some medical students from Dunoon came to help us. Granny had a broken leg and a head wound and died two weeks later in Killearn Hospital. My mother and I had head wounds. We thank God we survived but have never been able to thank the people who helped us.

My parents had Granny's name, Mrs Hannah Ahern, inserted in the Book of Remembrance in Edinburgh Castle – she is in the Stirling part because of where she died. My sister, aged eight, was taken by neighbours to another shelter, where we later found her.

Mary Brockway (née Armstrong, from New Brunswick)

WALTER BROWN'S

The night of the thirteenth of March I had been working at Walter Brown's (Draper) shop at 20 Dumbarton Road where I had been transferred a year or so before. The shop I had been in at 674 Dumbarton Road was completely destroyed in the ensuing Blitz.

After work, my friend and co-worker Jean Young and I went to a movie in Glasgow. On the way home by bus, the raid had already started and the driver would not go further than Yoker. So we trooped off the bus and proceeded to walk home. Scenes of devastation were all around but we kept walking and taking shelter when bombs came whistling down. When we reached Kilbowie Road, for some unknown reason, we each went our own way, Jean to Dalmuir where she lived in Pattison Street, and I off up Kilbowie Road to try and reach Albert Road where I lived. I remember climbing over a huge crater and sheltering in a close near the new Cinema (the La Scala). I heard the whistle of the bomb that destroyed it. When I finally reached home at around 6 o'clock, the all-clear had sounded. Our house had been destroyed and those of my brothers. My dear mother had been ill for six months before the Blitz and Dr Allan had ordered her to leave Clydebank. So she and my dad went to Newmilns, Ayrshire and were there that night. Mother told me afterwards she had prayed for the people of Clydebank and her family. She read the 91st Psalm and was comforted by those wonderful promises of our God.

Moya Horton (from British Columbia)

NEVER TO RETURN

My sister Audrey and I shared a bedroom with a huge window on a top floor. At that time I was working in a dress shop and she was finishing a Commercial course in a college. My father had been sent to London – it was supposed to be temporary. That night we heard the planes and got out of bed to look out the window. It was a beautiful night with a clear sky. We looked up and saw searchlights shining on the plane. That scared us, so we both jumped into clothes and ran across the road to people who gathered in a downstairs flat. We all sat in a large hall with the doors around us closed, and the ladies had tea and cake.

Then there was a terrible bang and we all clung to one another. We waited some time and then a silence came When I got up to go home, a gentleman said to me, 'Moya, sit down.' Then he held my hand and told me our flat was not safe to enter. We were taken to school turned into a shelter. Next day we were allowed into our flat to see the damage and clean up the glass from the windows smashed the night before. The street was cordoned off and everyone came from all around to gaze at the damaged houses. Now this is the night before the big blitz.

I had two maiden aunts (quite well off) and Audrey and I went there for meals and to sleep. Late that night the sirens sounded and we went to the shelter in my aunts' apartment block. It was a long night. All of Greenock was hit that night, all but the West end where we were. The bombs the night before had been the only ones in that district. In Greenock, the railway line was damaged, the telephones were out, the bus depot was hit, the gas was out, ships were torn out of the shipyards, tenements were demolished. It was a frightful night.

I had to get in touch with my dad to say we were alright. So I went to the main street out of town and I got a lift on a potato lorry to Port Glasgow, about 25 miles away. I went to a government office and there a man that had golfed with my dad got me through to London. I spoke to my father and told him I was taking the next train to London – which was a few days because the main line was out of service. My married sister moved into our flat and Audrey and I packed our belongings and left our home for ever and ever.

Lily Taddeo(from Niagra, N.Y.)

340 DUMBARTON ROAD

The two days – March 13 and 14 – are certainly etched in my mind. At that time, I lived in the top flat at 340 Dumbarton Road. These were moonlight nights as I recall. I believe when we heard the sirens we thought it would be the usual 'hit and run,' but that's not how it worked out. I was fifteen years old. I recall when my parents and I joined our neighbours down in the close, wondering if the next hit was for us. I recall the fear in the voices and on the faces of those gathered on those nights. But my mother, bless her, was brave. If she was fearful, she did not display it. After the two nightmare nights, we all bundled up a few belongings and went out to Dumbarton Road where we hitched a ride with any passing lorry that would take us.

Alasdair Galloway

GOOD CAN COME OUT OF BAD

On the night of 13th March, my mother, Laura McCormack and father, William Galloway had been to see 'Gone with the Wind' in Glasgow, and were coming home on the bus when they heard the air raid sirens go off. Shortly after, the first bombs started to fall. My father wanted to see my mother home (they were at the time – in local vocabulary – 'winching'), but she convinced him to stay on the bus and she got off at the stop opposite her tenement close in Glasgow Road. The bus carried on with bombs exploding all around until Gavinburn Bus Garage when the driver said that he was going no further. My father, though, was fortunate to get a lift home to Dumbarton from a passing motorist.

My mother meantime, and for the rest of the night, was standing in the close with her mother and the other residents. Her own father was on night shift in the Co-op bakery in Elgin Street. Neither knew the other was safe until the morning. It's difficult to appreciate how terrifying it must have been standing in the pitch dark with bombs exploding all around and never knowing when the one might fall that had your name on it. It really only came to me one day in 1983, when my mother had come down to see her grandson in our house in Dumbarton. We live round the corner from the local Fire Station which, at that time, summoned its reserve firemen by sounding the air-raid siren. At the first sound of the siren, the colour drained from my mother's face. I asked her if she was alright. She said, 'I'll be fine. It just brings it all back sometimes.'

On the morning of the 14th March, my mother made her way to work at Cumbernauld Primary School. Teaching jobs were difficult to come by at that time and she was usually anxious to keep on the Headmaster's right side. However, with the devastating events of the previous night, despite her best efforts, she arrived late. Her class was being taken by another teacher (along with her own, something like 100 children) who greeted her with the message that the Headmaster wanted to see her. Walking along to his office, she told me, that she thought: 'right, I'm going to really tell him about this, and how lucky he is that I'm even here.'

However, when she got to the office, she was greeted with: 'It's O.K. You're not here for a row. In fact, I can't tell you how pleased I am to see you. I heard about what happened in Clydebank last night. Mr Leadbeater [the local minister] has been up to say that if I knew of anyone from Clydebank who needed shelter, just to send them round to the manse. So, off you go back to Clydebank and get your family and your things, and we'll see you tomorrow!'

The upshot of this was not only that my mother and her family had much needed shelter – since their home, like so many, was uninhabitable – but also it forged a friendship that lasted for many years afterwards. Good can come out of bad!

Mary Dyer

POOR GARGOYLE

We lived in a house in the High street in Dumbarton. It had three storeys and we lived at the top. We had no shelter but the close was strutted with metal bars and there were canvas curtains came down at either end to close it off. There were wooden benches where we sat along the side, and there was what was called a baffle wall which was built in the middle of the pavement in front of every close along the High Street – and caused more damage to the pedestrians than the Germans ever did, because, in the blackout, people forgot they were there and walked into them with great regularity

We had a system where, as soon as the air raid siren went, the people that lived on the top moved down to the second floor and picked up the people that lived there and then we went down to the first floor flat and we all stayed in there until such time as the elders decided that it was time to go down to the close, which was naturally very cold and draughty. I would be nine at this time and we had our siren suits that we were bundled into. And the case with all the insurance policies and the birth certificates was duly lugged along beside us.

On the 13th of March 1941, it was very, very noisy. You could hear the aeroplanes and, constantly through the night, the sound of breaking glass. I never knew there was as much glass in the world as crashed that night.

As it so happened, it was my father's birthday. He was an A.R.P. warden and he was out doing his rounds when, about half past two, in the morning, my younger sister who would be seven at the time, suddenly woke up from a sleep and announced to all and sundry that Hitler hadn't forgotten her daddy's birthday.

I remember at one point having to go outside, and I was allowed to go out the back way. The washing green, what was referred to as 'the green', ran right down to the river. Then on the other side of the river was Levengrove Park. All the grass on our side was burning, Part of the river was burning, and all of the buildings in Weir Terrace were burning. It was just like as if night had been turned into day.

We had an incident later on, about six o'clock in the morning, when all of a sudden there was this whistling sound, the sound we imagined would be a bomb falling. Everyone was told to throw themselves on to the floor, which they did. And nothing happened. So after about half an hour we were allowed to sit up. But no-one would venture outside. Then, about half past seven, we did go outside when it was light, and we discovered that what we had thought was a bomb was a gargoyle from the church next door. It had come whistling down and hit the pavement. And there it was, the poor gargoyle, lying in the gutter.

Mary Wood

EVACUATION TO STENHOUSEMUIR

On the 13th of March, Dad decided we would just stay in the cupboard at the foot of the stairs as he was fed up with going to the shelter every time the sirens went off. However, my mother said no, we were going to the shelter. Which was just as well because one of the bombs landed on that part of the house.

When morning came, we came out of the shelter to find our house badly damaged. We couldn't get into it at all. So my mother told my father to take us up to the Hardgate where his parents and sisters lived. After he left us, he came back down to the house. He managed to prop up a plank of wood against the wall and get in through a broken window and found our budgie still alive.

On the evening of the 14th we spent another night, in a shelter in Hardgate, listening to the bombs dropping. The next day we were all evacuated and spent our first night in Kippen and next morning on to Stenhousemuir where we were allocated rooms in the houses of people who had volunteered to take us in. During our stay, I left school and got a job in Carron Company. I was then fourteen.

My father, as well as my uncles, had to get back to work, so, he being a joiner, boarded up one of my aunt's houses and stayed there for a wee while. We only saw him at weekends.

My brother, who was in the army, got special leave when he heard of the Clydebank Blitz. He arrived in Clydebank and couldn't find us because my mother hadn't had time to let him know where we were. He got such a shock when he saw our house, not knowing if we had survived. Anyway, he made enquiries and came to Stenhousemuir to find us all alive, thanks to my mother.

When my mother told me it was time to leave as our house was ready, I wasn't too happy. I had made such a lot of good friends and I had blended into a new life. The people spoke with a country accent which I had picked up and I thought that we would be staying there forever. When I came home and got a job in the R.O.F. Dalmuir, my boss couldn't believe that I belonged to Clydebank. But I soon lost my new accent and found myself again, and a lot of new friends once more.

I still keep in touch with a lady whose grandparents had taken my grandparents into their home after the Blitz. I have a lot of memories of my stay in Stenhousemuir and if it hadn't been for the Clydebank Blitz I would never have met these people. But a lot of people must still have terrible memories and wish the Clydebank Blitz had never happened.

Janet Nairn

MY LOST SCHOOLING

I was eleven years old on March 13th 1941, a beautiful, bright moonlight night. I lived with my father, mother and two sisters, in a little village named Hardgate on the outskirts of Clydebank. I attended the local school in Duntocher.

We had been prepared for air-raids. An Anderson shelter had been erected in our garden, and we had used it on several occasions. But on that night, everything happened so quickly, we did not manage to get to the shelter, so had to remain in the house. My father went upstairs to bring my grandfather and grandmother down to our house. Then he got us all to sit in the lobby as he thought this would be the safest place, as there were no windows and two external doors.

Everything was fine until a landmine fell on the Duntocher Hosiery Mill a short distance from our house and the explosion forced open the two doors and shattered the windows. My father had then to barricade the doors with furniture to keep them closed. By now, he realised how serious the raid was and obviously the target was Clydebank. During a lull he went outside for a look around and saw the red glow in the sky from the burning fires. By this time, we were concerned as we had family living in Clydebank.

In the morning when the all-clear sounded, we realised the amount of damage that had been done. A landmine had fallen on our village and two families, six adults and one child, who had been in their shelters had been killed and their homes demolished. This place has been grassed over and never built on.

On the Friday night we were prepared to go to the shelter, and by this time, my uncle, aunt and two cousins were with us as their house had been damaged by a bomb. On Saturday morning, throughout the village, windows were shattered, ceilings were down and the gas supply had been cut off. It was decided to evacuate the people. Buses arrived and took us to a school in Kippen where we stayed overnight. Next morning we were allocated places to go. We were very lucky and were offered accommodation with a very nice couple in Stenhousemuir.

My father and sister worked in the Singer factory, so they had a lot of travelling there and back. But as soon as the damage to our house had been repaired, we returned to our home. This was when I found out how much this would affect me. There was no school for me to go to. Our minister, Rev. Moses Cochrane, held a class for us in the church hall, but I did not return to school until after the summer holiday. I had just moved into my Qualifying Exam class in February, so my education was badly disrupted. When I did return to school, I had to travel with my school friends to Hartfield School in Dumbarton. This meant a tram and train journey to and from school. And what a difference this school was from the small village school I had attended. It was so big, with so many rooms and corridors. Different teachers for each class. I thought I would never find my way around. But eventually, I settled in. One of the good things I remember was that, as I had a packed lunch, I had time to queue at the little shop that sold home-made toffee and buy a poke of toffee to take home to share with my younger sister.

Eventually, I returned to Clydebank Junior Secondary School and remained there until I left school at fourteen and started my first job in an office. As I had no Higher education, I went to Skerry's College in Glasgow two evenings a week and took a course in Shorthand/Typing, and eventually, I got a secretarial job.

Claire Kennedy (née MacDonald)

GETTING TO WORK

It was a Thursday night and my brother Frank had arrived home on leave unexpectedly earlier in the day. During the war, servicemen could not let their families know when they'd be getting leave. Frank had been abroad, serving in the Royal Navy, which he had joined in 1937 at the age of eighteen.

We were sitting in our home at 12 Livingstone Street when the sirens went off. I suggested making supper. We were in the top flat of the tenement, and at the top of the building there was a domed glass roof. As I went into the kitchen, I lifted the teapot. There was suddenly an awful blast, and such a dreadful sound of breaking glass. I don't know yet whether it was the blast or sheer fright, but the teapot just disappeared. It just shot out of my hand.

My mother and father, Frank, brothers Jim (15) and Brendan (8) and I gathered in the lobby. When we stepped out on to the landing, we thought the stairway had collapsed. Frank investigated and found it was the debris from the roof which was covering the stair. So we were able to climb over it and make our way downstairs.

The rest of the night, we spent in the close, listening to the bombs whistling down with such terrible force. You were always expecting the next one to hit the building. There were three families on each landing, and the building was three storeys high. As the night progressed other people joined us, usually in a lull in the bombing. Some were running to escape from a burning building, and others were making their way home, dodging in and out of the closes. One family arrived with a young baby. My father climbed back over the rubble at the top of the stairs to fetch some milk from our house. I remember him lighting a candle, and putting the pan containing the milk over it to heat it up to feed the baby.

The next day was spent contacting relatives (two lots of aunts and uncles) to make sure we were all accounted for. Frank, being on leave, had to report that morning back to Greenock, where his ship was berthed.

On the Friday night, we left Clydebank and made our way to the countryside, up to the Girnin Gates. When the sirens went off a farmer offered us his Anderson shelter, where we all spent that night (aunts and uncles included).

On Saturday morning, after the all-clear, we proceeded home again and thankfully the house was still there, but no water or electricity. First thing was to get a sleep as we were all exhausted. My brother Frank arrived back and told us that his shipmates had been under orders not to fire at the waves of German planes the previous two nights in case it would draw attention to the shipyards and the ships berthed at Greenock.

That day, we were told to use buses that were laid on and leave Clydebank altogether. You just had to join one and take pot luck. Our destination was Helensburgh. Saturday and Sunday we spent in Clyde Street School, Helensburgh, sleeping on the floor until the locals offered their homes. They usually took either two brothers or two sisters who could share a room.

On the road to Helensburgh the burning oil tanks at Dalnottar had caused a blockage on the road, so the bus made a detour through the field and got stuck in the mud, and we all had to get out. I think the men managed to push the bus back on to the road.

It had been a hurried evacuation because they said there was an unexploded bomb near the building. My mother was still wearing her slippers when we arrived at Helensburgh. We found out where the nearest church was , and made our way to the service on Sunday.

I was working in the Clydebank Co-op Central Grocers in Alexander Street, and I checked in for work as usual at 8 a.m. on the Monday, having travelled up by bus from Helensburgh. I remember they had a list with our names on it and scored you off once you reported for work. I also remember some workmen who worked in Brown's but lived in Glasgow coming in and trying it on, saying they had been bombed out and claiming extra rations.

My sister Kathleen and I were billeted with a nice couple, a schoolmaster and his wife who had a daughter aged twenty. But after a few weeks Kathleen and I wanted home. On the first night of the Blitz, Kathleen had been going out of the close to go to the night shift in Brown's when the first bomb fell across the street. She just carried on her way, as she knew she had to get to her work.

Evacuees queuing for buses in Whitecrook Street

David Dyer

A SERIES OF MENTAL PICTURES

I lived with my mother and brother in a tenement building in Windsor Place in Bowling. On the night of the Clydebank Blitz, there was also an Italian family called Utini in the house with us. The building was bombed and it collapsed, and my mother and myself were buried for thirty six hours. My brother John, who was ten years old, was killed. Granny Utini was also killed. The reason, I believe, that my brother was killed was that he was sitting beside the fire along with Granny Utini. And I and another child were under the table. I've been told that an incendiary bomb came down the chimney. And that was the blast that blew the house apart and killed my brother.

I sustained multiple bruising and shock, and my mother had severely damaged her leg. We subsequently ended up in Robroyston Hospital and one of the first mental pictures is of me playing in a ward and seeing the head doctor walking about the ward followed by two dachshund dogs.

The next picture I have in my mind is standing on a table in Bank Street in Alexandria wearing a wee pair of woolly knickers and a woolly semmit and being dressed in navy blue shorts, a navy blue jumper with a blue stripe, a tie with horizontal bars, socks, boots, a trench coat, a skull cap, a small suitcase with one or two belongings, and a Mickey Mouse gas mask. And a label tied round my neck, stamped 'Evacuee'. We were then taken over to the station and I was evacuated to Ardrishaig.

I have only one or two pictures of Ardrishaig in my mind. There were four children in the house where we lived. We were looked after by what I thought was an old lady, she could have been anything between forty and sixty, I just don't remember. I remember the oldest boy was about twelve and he, very sadly, was drowned in Ardrishaig, in the harbour.

I spent eighteen months in Ardrishaig, till the time I was ready to go back to school. I was then sent back to the Renton because I had an aunt who lived there, and my mother was being discharged from Robroyston.

When I started in the Renton Public School I was the only child who got Red Cross parcels from America. I have a very strong mental picture of opening a box in the school. There was a toy Santa full of jelly babies, and a box of soap powder. And they both had burst. And all the jelly babies were mixed up in the soap powder.

After my father was discharged from the army, we were sent back to Bowling to live in temporary accommodation, because that's where we'd come from. I lived there till I started High School in Clydebank. Then, after my first year in Clydebank High, I returned to Dumbarton, and that's where I've been ever since.

Myra Brady

WOMEN CAME INTO THEIR OWN

The morning after the Blitz, when we went out into the main road, Cunard Street, all I saw was St James's Church facing me and all the dead bodies. It was pretty horrible. Coal lorries packing the bodies into them. And I always remember that when they were packing them into the lorries, I actually saw somebody move. Now whether they were dead or not dead, it frightened the wits out of me and I never forgot it. I used to dream about it, quite often for a long, long time afterwards.

We left there and went to stay in Kirkintilloch. Our house was bomb damaged, but we were able to come back and collect as many wee things as we could. And then my mother and father gradually went back to the house, though it wasn't really fit. I had a job in Barr and Stroud's in a shadow factory out in Kirkintilloch. They used part of the foundry, called the Lion Foundry, as an instrument-making factory, making prisms and things for the range finders. It was hush-hush. So, I stayed on in Kirkintilloch because I had this boyfriend that I had met in the factory, and eventually ended up getting married to him.

Later on in the war, I joined up in the Civil Defence, full-time, and after that I went to St John's of Jerusalem. In the Civil Defence, I was an ambulance driver. I was supposed to be, but actually I used to drive the staff officers around to their different depots all over the place. I would have said that was a good war for me! But it was a horrible war for a lot of people.

Women came into their own during the war. Men discovered that women were as good as them. I had an aunt who worked as a welder in John Brown's. Women came out of their shell. They never had a chance previous to that.

Friends of ours were completely wiped out in the Blitz. I had a friend, Margaret McLean. She lived in Shaftesbury Street in Dalmuir and I was supposed to go down to her house that night. But when I came home from work, I was too tired to be bothered. So I never went. Well, that night, there was only Margaret and her mother in the house – the rest of the family were on the night shift. They went into the air-raid shelter and it got a direct hit. So if I'd gone, I could have been there along with them.

We never lost anyone in my own family, but we had a lot of nervous wrecks after it. I think my mother never really got over it. She never did, because she used to wake up during the night just touching us all to see if we were alright. Things like that.

Sheila Munn

THE 1939 EVACUATIONS

In 1939 many children were evacuated to what were considered safer areas – about 8-10 miles away! While this may have seemed like a good idea, many adults did not seem to have any inkling of the psychological damage they were possibly inflicting on young children who did not have any real understanding as to why they were being sent away from their homes and known surroundings. The children were taken to their local station where they were duly labelled and put on the train. Why no adult member of their own family was allowed to accompany them to see where they were going seemed strange and, indeed, how did their relatives eventually find out where their children were boarded.

As one of those children, I can recall sitting huddled miserably in a corner of the carriage in utter bewilderment with my gas mask and few belongings on my knee waiting to see who would pick me and where I would be taken! As the train pulled into Cardross station, the platform was lined with many ladies who went among the children choosing the ones they would like to foster. Imagine the children of today, who are told not to trust anyone unknown to them, being taken off a train by a total stranger and taken to some unknown house! The wife of my schoolmaster from Clydebank eventually chose the girl from next door and myself, and we duly arrived at a lovely detached stone house in Cardross. I wish that I possessed such a property today but under very different and happier conditions.

Some children were happy in their new surroundings, though most were not, perhaps due to the circumstances of their arrival or the fact that some of the foster families were doing their wartime duty under some duress. With hindsight, perhaps it could safely be said that the whole idea, while done with the best of intentions, was a dreadful mistake. As it turned out, almost all of these children were back in there own homes before the real hostilities began. It was probably a better gamble that they chanced death with their own families in the more industrial areas rather than being left as orphans with strangers in the country who would, no doubt, have immediately put them into an orphanage had their natural parents been killed.

Ruby Stewart

THE HIGH PARK

In 1941 I was a young woman of twenty seven, three years married, and we lived at 84 Second Avenue, the end close. That Thursday, 13th March, we had a friend from London home on his first leave from the Air Force. He and his wife invited me for dinner at Lewis's (he had been a salesman there). My husband was working late in the ordnance factory in Dalmuir, so he could not be there. We had a lovely dinner then afternoon tea at Fraser's.

I left my friends in Glasgow at 5 p.m., ready to go to an A.R.P. training meeting after teatime. We were going to go over gas mask drill, which we had done before. Then the sirens went, but all of us in the Town Hall were quite relaxed about it. There had been previous warnings of air raids. They usually lasted about two hours or so, with nothing happening. So we were walking home, quite happy, when the action started.

We began to hear the bombs falling – then we heard the guns from the Polish ships (in Brown's). They kept on firing till the guns were empty. We got to our close and then went to the shelter across the road on the drying green. It was built above ground with a concrete half-circle roof. About 12.45 a.m., the landmine came down and hit the middle of our building. Nobody in our close was killed, although a young couple and their baby in the next close were killed, plus another seventy people out of our block of six closes.

After that, the wardens came along and asked all who could walk to make their way to the High Park. They said the planes would not drop bombs on an open Park. And they didn't. We were advised to lie flat whenever we heard anything descending. We spent the next five hours or so up there.

On the way there I met a woman carrying a child, about 3, on her back, and she also had a young infant in her arms. The child could not walk as she had hurt her foot. I took the baby – it was just three days old the woman told me. It was one of twins, and the other twin had died. The mother said that this baby was now dying. I wrapped my Harris tweed coat round it, but I felt it stiffen and die in my arms.

In the High Park, the scenes were terrible. People were running about hysterical, looking for other people. Nobody had any warm clothing with them. It was a bitterly cold night and we just had to stretch out on the grass without any covering. I saw St. Stephen's being hit. Bits of the building flew up in the air – girders looking like matchsticks. The Catholic people who saw this were in an awful state, seeing their lovely church suffering like that.

Back at the Holy City our building was cordoned off on the Friday morning. My mother in Whitecrook sent a wee boy to look for us, and when he came back, he said there was nothing left of our building. My mother was in a terrible state. There was a neighbouring family with one of the boys away in Borstal. He was the sole survivor of the family – his mother and his five brothers were killed that night. I met him in Clydebank after the Blitz. He said, 'I'm all alone now.' I felt very sorry him, and walked up the road a bit with him. I understand that the boy was eventually taken in by relatives in Ireland.

My husband had been working late that night and then he was out on A.R.P. duty. In the morning, he found his parents safe in Radnor Park Bowling Club. His father, Grandpa Stewart, was a great old boy. He had an artificial leg, but, even with that, he was known to tap dance at times.

On the Friday, my husband and I, his parents and my parents, all went to Holytown, a mining community, in David Ballantyne's coal lorry (he had hosed it down). It was a very different sort of life there. My husband had to travel up to Clydebank daily for his work.

In May 1941, we had a grand reunion of Clydebank folk in the Hamilton Palais. We met folk we didn't know had survived. In 1942 the government made a rule that if you had no children you had to work. I had been a machine operator before I married, but this time I worked in Singer's general store. A few months later I found I was pregnant, so I left in October, and my son was born in December 1942.

William Bowman

FIRST AID

I was on duty as shift head of First Aid in the ambulance room at Beardmore Diesels, Dalmuir, on the night of the Blitz at Clydebank.

The factory was hit by several bombs and there were many casualties. The head of the firefighters and myself went out into the factory to find the casualties and bring them into the First Aid Room, which was reinforced. Once the casualties were treated, I ran up Beardmore Street (Dalmuir) to go to the Ambulance Station, which was in Dalmuir School. However, I met an ambulance at the top of the road. The ambulance was in fact a canvas-covered truck fitted to take four stretchers. I stood on the running board of the vehicle to guide the driver past bomb craters and debris. The ambulance arrived and we had just loaded the first casualty into it when we heard the whistle of a bomb. We threw ourselves to the ground as the bomb fell. It hit a sewer, and part of the heavy sewer cover tore through the canvas of the truck and killed the man lying on the stretcher inside. Another ambulance came and the rest of the injured were removed to hospital.

After the all-clear, I went into Clydebank to check that my parents were alright. Not an easy journey! As I was a member of the Civil Defence Casualty Service – a Red Cross volunteer – I made my way to the First Aid post in Elgin Street School. I was sent to the Episcopal Church on Glasgow Road to find out the situation as many people were gathered there, most suffering with eye complaints caused by whitewash and plaster from ceilings and walls getting in to their eyes – this contained lime and caused a very painful condition. I returned to the First Aid Post to arrange transport to take them to the Eye Infirmary.

On the second night of the Blitz, as I went to report for duty at the H.Q. of the local Civil Defence, which was in Clydebank Library, part of the tenement just along the road was blown into the street. A dispatch rider took me along to the Elgin Street post, which was operating at first from the air-raid shelters in the playground. Most casualties that night were firemen as most civilians had been evacuated. Later we moved to the basement of the Clydebank Co-operative Biscuit Factory, which was opposite the school. Here we had water, lighting and accommodation that we did not have in the shelter. But, by then there was very little first aid material left – swabs, cotton wool, dressings, etc. Needles were boiled in a pan on a Primus stove. Most firemen after treatment went straight back on duty.

The street where I lived was badly damaged by one of the first 'stick of bombs' that fell. The whole of the back of the building was blown out. Some furniture and personal belongings were later recovered by the Salvage Service. The destruction left me without a home and with only the clothes that I was wearing. I felt helpless, dirty and hungry – though the Salvation Army quickly set up a snack bar the following day.

I was evacuated with my parents to Kilbarchan on Saturday, 15th March. This meant about an hour or more of journey to and from work – the journey had to be made on buses and the Renfrew Ferry, so timing was difficult. There was, for a while, a special cheap bus ticket for evacuated workers. Every other night I stayed in Clydebank on duty at the First Aid Post (in the basement of the Co-op Bakery).

Rena Nimmo (née Fleming)

COUNTRY EVACUATION

After the second night of the bombing we returned to Burns Street to find nothing left of our home. All that remained was a pile of rubble, a lot of smoke and many dead. The bottom half of our side of the street had had a direct hit and the whole street was cordoned off.

We were homeless and were left with the few belongings we had taken with us. Going on to Mount Blow we discovered that my other grandparents' house had suffered a similar fate. Gran Fleming told the story of being in the shelter at the bottom of the garden with the family. Smelling burning and remembering that she had left soup simmering on the cooker she insisted that she would go back to switch the power off. On looking out, they discovered that it was the house that was burning.

We had to return to the house in Bearsden where we stayed for several more nights until traced by relatives who took us back to their small flat in Rutherglen.

Since it was obvious that we couldn't stay indefinitely in the limited accommodation in Rutherglen it was decided that my Gran Bell and I should go for a short stay with a relative and her family on a farm on the hillside above the village of Gateside in Fife. My schooling could then continue in the two-teacher Gateside Primary. Shortly after our arrival my grandmother became quite ill and was taken to Perth Royal Infirmary for what was to be a fairly lengthy stay. Since it was impossible for me to remain where I was without my grandmother, and my mother was still trying to find somewhere to stay in Dalmuir, I became a true evacuee with label and small case.

The authorities arranged for me to stay with a shepherd and his wife who lived on a fairly remote farm called Easter Gospetry above the village of Burnside just into Kinross-shire. Like the people in Bearsden, they had little choice in the matter. They had to take either two boys or one girl because they had the accommodation. Luckily they chose me. Bob and Peggy Millar provided a haven from the upheaval of the previous weeks and my stay there lasted for three happy years.

Life at Easter Gospetry couldn't have been more different from the one I knew and there followed a difficult few months adjustment for all of us. For a 'townie' like me it took time to get used to the country way of life. No gas or electricity – cooking was done on a range backing on to the sitting room fire; grocery shopping was done on a fortnightly visit to Milnathort which involved a twenty – thirty minute walk to the main road to catch the bus for a fifteen minute journey to town. The baker and butcher vans called once or twice a week and the post van came daily.

When we were snowed up, provisions and mail were left in a box for that purpose at the end of the rough road leading up to the farm. It was a lonely life for a six-year-old used to the tenement way of life with plenty of friends around, trams almost on the doorstep and plenty of shops. There was only the one house at Easter Gospetry for the shepherd, and a bothy used infrequently for seasonal workers. My lifeline was going to school which involved the long walk to the main road in all weathers, depositing the 'wellies' at a friend's house and taking the bus for the ten minute or so ride to Gateside Primary. I loved it there and made many friends. Of course, when the snow was too deep it meant an unexpected holiday from school as I would have disappeared into a snowdrift long before I reached the main road!

For the Millars too it wasn't an easy time. They were a childless couple. Bob Millar was already in his sixties and his wife, Peggy, was twenty years younger with no experience of children. Nevertheless, they took on this extra task as they took on everything else, with a will to make it work and extreme kindness. Thus started a friendship which lasted until Peggy Millar died six years ago in her nineties.

Although life was solitary in many ways, I had plenty of animals around. Always a pet lamb or two following me around. I remember the excitement of the new-born lambs being thawed out by the fire and bottle-fed by me when there was no mother to take care of them

The day started early for the Millars at around 5.30 a.m. when the cow had to be milked – something I tried to do with little success! Naturally it was early to bed. With paraffin lamps in the main rooms and a candle quickly extinguished when I was safely in bed, it's just as well that I wasn't afraid of the dark.

Apart from the lack of company of other children on the farm, the thing I missed most was the lack of music which was part of everyday life at home. The accumulator (battery) for the radio was too precious to waste so the radio was only on for important things like the news. On Sundays, it wasn't on at all and the minimum of work was done. We never went to church because there was no transport there and back, but Bob Millar read the bible.

There were compensations, however. They were fairly self sufficient at Easter Gospetry. There was an extensive garden with all the vegetables needed and fruits in season. Peggy Millar made her own butter, jams and was one of the best bakers that I ever met. (I still use her recipes today). There were lots of hens so plenty of eggs were available as well as the odd roast chicken to eat and ham if a pig was slaughtered. It's no wonder that soon I became a slightly tubbier version of the little girl who had left Dalmuir a few months before!

The education in school was excellent so I suffered no ill effects in that area. My teacher, who was also the head teacher, kept in touch long after I had gone back home and left me silver teaspoons when she died many years later.

While I was at the farm, Italian then German prisoners stayed in the Bothy while working on the farm. At first they were brought daily but eventually stayed there. There were two Italians in particular, who spring to mind. They insisted on doing their laundry at a water trough in the yard and generally rejected offers of cooked food and other comforts. One of them said that he was good at decorating and started to distemper the sitting room in a creamy colour. 'Stippling' seemed to be in at the time and he said that he would do this in a chocolate brown (I think that these were the two colours available). Unfortunately he was in a particularly bad mood that day and his attempt at stippling was large brown blobs all over the walls as if someone had been playing football against it with a muddy ball. Disaster! It was something the Millars had to live with for a long time! As Peggy Millar was extremely houseproud, you can guess how this affected her.

Several German prisoners stayed in the Bothy, two of whom kept in touch after the war. One Alois Brendel, stayed on after the war and only returned to Germany when his elderly father became ill and he needed to return home.

In 1952, a few years after Bob Millar's death, Peggy and I went to Hanover on a visit to Alois. How I marvelled at the rapid post-war building that was taking place there. They were so far ahead of Clydebank it seemed strange since we had won the war!

Alois is now in his seventies, stays in the same place in Hanover and writes a long letter to me at the beginning of every year.

I returned home to Dalmuir in 1944. My mother had, by this time, been rehoused in Mount Blow, my father was in Burma and my brother had been born in April of that year. I gather that the arrival of the baby changed everything. My mother came to the farm on a visit with the new baby to let me see him and I kicked up such a fuss when they were leaving without me that I had to be taken with them!

Thinking back, I caused great heartache to that lovely couple who had wanted to adopt me and it could have been the end of a beautiful friendship. But no, I continued to see them regularly, spending most of the long summer holidays there, sometimes taking other friends with me. When Bob Millar died, Peggy moved to Aberdour, Fife where she stayed until going into a home outside Dunfermline. She died there in 1991.

Helen McNeill

REMEMBERING THOSE WHO DIED IN THE BLITZ

My mother's family were killed on the 13th March 1941. The bodies of those killed were never found and any remains of those bodies were buried in the communal grave at Dalnottar Cemetery in Dalmuir. As there were no funerals, my mother felt that she had never said goodbye and had no grave to tend. Therefore she relied on the communal grave as a special place for her to visit when she felt sad and unhappy.

She loved the fact that each year on the Saturday morning nearest to the 13th of March a service of remembrance was held and the Provost of the town laid a wreath and many of the town's officials attended. For fifty years Mum attended this service. Come hail, rain, sleet or snow, she was at

Blitz Memorial Service in 1997: Helen McNeill with her mother and Rev. Archie Pearson

the graveside. When, after the fiftieth anniversary of the Blitz, the town council decided to discontinue this service, my mother was distraught. She could not believe the service was to be stopped, yet we were still as a nation remembering armistice day for the 1914 – 18 war.

I told her we would continue to go and we spoke to a few others. Together we decided we would continue the service on our own. We approached the clergy, Canon James McShane and Rev. Archie Pearson as they both had been conducting the service for many years, and they agreed to continue, as did the piper Willie Gough, who played a lament at the end of the service. Seven years on this act of remembrance is still taking place. Sadly though, Willie Gough has since died and his friend and colleague Maurice Pert agreed to take his place. We know that the people who still attend the service each year are delighted that it still takes place.

In 1997, Kilbowie St. Andrews Church celebrated its centenary by dedicating part of the church to be a Blitz Memorial Chapel. In the chapel is a book of remembrance with the names of the people who died on the 13th – 14th March 1941.

But these are deeds which should not pass away
And names that must not wither.

Byron

The Tapestry by Helen McNeill at The Blitz Memorial Chapel, Kilbowie St. Andrew's Parish Church, Clydebank

Ann Holmes (daughter of Annie Rocks and Walter Greig)

THE ROCKS FAMILY

The night the German bombers struck Clydebank, I lived with my mother, father and sisters, Susan and Mary in the bottom flat of 5 Kitchener Street, Dalmuir West. Across the backcourt lived my grandparents, uncles, aunts and cousins at 78 Jellicoe Street. The family name was Rocks and it suffered the greatest loss of any family in Britain in the Blitz. On the night of 13th – 14th March, we lost four generations of the family: my great grandmother, grandmother, uncles, aunts and cousins.

The night started with my sisters and I being put to bed. As the sirens started, my mother and father lifted us from the bed and placed the three of us in the lobby sitting on the coal bunker. They covered us in blankets and put coats all around us to protect us from blasts or shrapnel from the bombs. At that point, they did not make their way to the Anderson Shelter that had been built in the backcourt. When the sirens started that night, many people wondered if it was a genuine air-raid as there had been a few false alarms over the past week. As the noise of the guns started and we could hear the bombs beginning to fall, our neighbours from upstairs came down to our house, as they considered it safer there. There were therefore eight families in our house – mothers, fathers, children. There were some people hiding under the kitchen table, children crying and wetting the floor in fright, other people being sick. So my mother and father were busy clearing up after them and coming into the lobby to check on Susan, Mary and me to make sure we were safe.

During all the commotion, my mother's brother, John, came into the house. He had been to the dancing in Glasgow, and had to walk from Yoker to get home, as all the transport had been halted there. He had called to make sure we were alright before making his way to Jellicoe Street. He spoke to me and Mary and Susan in the hall, laughing and making fun of all the coats around us, asking if we were playing at wee houses, making us laugh playing peekaboo with him. I needed to go to the toilet at that time, so my uncle took me. I remember looking at the top of the toilet window and seeing the sky red. I was very frightened and asked my uncle why it was red as it was night time. He told me God was polishing up the sun to make it a nice day tomorrow and I was not to worry. After returning me on to the bunker and covering me again, he told my mother he was going home. My mother begged him to stay until the bombing finished, but he insisted on going home to make sure the family were alright in Jellicoe Street. My uncle never saw the sun in the morning. He was killed that night.

By this time, the bombing had got heavier and it was decided everyone would go outside into the Anderson Shelter as it might be safer there. My mother lifted my youngest sister Mary and things she thought we might need. My father lifted Susan and also took blankets to keep us warm and some food and clothing. He told me to stay where I was and he would be back for me in a minute – the shelter was close to the back close. But I did not obey him. I climbed up on to the kitchen draining board to see where he was and there I saw the bombs starting to fall over Jellicoe Street. At that moment, my father grabbed me from the window and ran back to the shelter with me. There we sat along with our neighbours huddled together for support and strength from each other as the bombs fell around us.

At my grandmother's house in Jellicoe Street, as well as the family, there were three friends – Mary McLaughlin, John McCormick and Jean Gibson. Mary McLaughlin was engaged to my Uncle Francis. They were to be married in June. She died that night, as did John McCormick. Jean Gibson told my mother later that, when the sirens started, my great grandmother said she was not going into any shelter as she had been there before and nothing had happened, so she would stay in the house. My grandmother would not leave her mother and the rest of the family would not leave their mother. So no-one went to the shelter. At 78 Jellicoe Street two Rocks families lived next door to each other. My mother's eldest brother Pat and his wife Bessie and their five children had managed to get a house there. My Uncle Pat worked beside my grandfather at Beardmore's, Dalmuir across the canal from where they lived. He was due to go on nightshift, but had asked my grandfather to change shifts, as when the sirens had gone before Bessie had panicked trying to get the children ready. So on that night, my grandfather was working and Pat stayed home with his family.

As the bombing got heavier, they also decided to go down to the bottom flat as it would be safer for them. At this point, Jean Gibson said she would go home to her own family. So, all the Rocks and Mary McLaughlin and John McCormick settled in the downstairs flat. My grandmother had taken Ann, one of her grandchildren on to her knee and was cuddling her. But their safety was shortlived, for a landmine made a direct hit on 78 Jellicoe Street, killing everyone. The uncle who left our house must have just entered 78 Jellicoe Street as the bomb exploded.

After the all-clear sounded and we came out of the shelter, my mother looked towards my grandmother's house and saw Jellicoe Street flattened. She started running, screaming for her mother, trying to move all the debris and rubble by hand, my father trying to pull her away, and Susan, Mary and I crying not knowing what was going on. When my father finally managed to get my mother home, he went to French Street to bring our granny over to look after us while he went to search the shelters to see if any of my mother's family were there. He told me years later, when we used to talk, that, as he searched that morning, he went into a shelter and there were five young girls sitting, arms linked, eyes open, all dead from a bomb blast. He said they looked as if they had been to the dancing and had taken shelter on their way home when the bombing started.

When he returned home, he was told all the Rocks family from Jellicoe Street were dead. My mother was devastated. Of her family, three survived – her father, her sister and herself. When my grandfather returned from work on the morning of 14th March, his mother-in-law, his wife, his sons Pat, James, John, Francis, Joseph and Thomas, his daughter Theresa, daughter-in-law Bessie, and five of his grandchildren were all dead, his home was totally destroyed and all he had was what he was wearing (working clothes).

That day we were evacuated to Helensburgh. We slept in a church hall for three days, lining up at The Granary to be fed. We were then housed

Some of the Rocks family a few years before the war: Patrick Rocks Senior is at the top right with his son Patrick in front of him. At the extreme left is Annie Grieg, née Rocks, the author's mother with her brother John in front of her.

with a family in Princes Street. Not wanting to leave us alone and giving us all the support he could, my father would walk from Helensburgh to Clydebank every day, as he worked in John Brown's. After doing a day's work, he would then make his way back to Helensburgh. During the day my mother would have heard that they had found some bodies or that someone was found walking about in a daze not knowing who they were. My mother would plead with my father to go and see if it was her family as they had not been found yet. She was also sure that her brother had not made it home that night and had lost his memory in the bomb blast and was wandering about. So my father would walk back to Clydebank again to make enquiries about anyone in hospital.

Eventually they got word that the families from Jellicoe Street had been found, and my grandfather would have to identify them as next of kin. My father went with my grandfather to help him through that ordeal. Again they had to go to all the places where the dead had been taken, looking at everybody that lay there. Finally at Hamilton Memorial Church they found what was left of the Rocks family. My grandfather managed to keep his composure until he came to his daughter Theresa, whose face had been blown apart. At that point my grandfather fainted. When he recovered he said he could not go on. My father asked if anyone else could identify them and was told no, it would have to be my grandfather and, if he could not go on, the ones he had not yet identified would have to go into the communal grave. As my grandfather carried on he wondered what my grandmother would be like after seeing Theresa. But he told us that when they saw my grandmother she looked as though she was sleeping. She still had my cousin Ann clasped in her arms. She must have instinctively held her tight as the bomb went off. And Ann was held tight as my grandmother was buried with her still clasped in her arms, the two of them together for ever. All are buried in Dalnottar Cemetery, some in two graves side by side and some in the communal grave.

In the days that followed, an application was made to the government to allow my grandfather to leave Scotland and go to Ireland away from Clydebank and his loss and to recover from the ordeal that our family had suffered. The request was granted and my grandfather, my mother, Susan, Mary and I sailed for Ireland. We landed in Belfast just as the Belfast Blitz started, so we lived the nightmare all over again. We were stranded in a train for three days, the people of Belfast being kind to all of us, bringing us food whenever they could. At last we settled down in the South of Ireland with relations of my grandfather, and it was over a year before I saw my father again when he was allowed to visit us. All of our lives were totally turned upside down through the bombing of Clydebank, and it has continued throughout my life.

Since then, my mother would visit the graveyard every year from the first anniversary of the Blitz, until her death in 1977, taking Susan, Mary and me with her. I promised my mother we would still honour the memorial every year. My sister Susan died in 1997 and now her daughters have taken their place beside me at the memorial service, as my daughters will take my place when my time comes. It is important to all of us that the Clydebank Blitz is never forgotten, not only for our family, but for